GOLDA MEIR

MOLLIE KELLER

GOLDA MEIR

FRANKLIN WATTS
NEW YORK I LONDON I TORONTO I SYDNEY I 1983
AN IMPACT BIOGRAPHY

A GROLIER COMPANY

9646

FOR MY MOTHER,
AND HERS

Cover photograph courtesy of
United Press International Photo

Photographs courtesy of
Zionist Archives and Library: pp. 12, 78, 85, 88, 95;
Consulate General of Israel: pp. 22, 36;
Pioneer Women: pp. 29, 47;
United Press International Photo: p. 110.

Library of Congress Cataloging in Publication Data

Keller, Mollie.
Golda Meir.

(An Impact biography)
Bibliography: p.
Includes index.
Summary: Traces the life and accomplishments of the woman Zionist
who at the age of seventy became the prime minister of Israel.
1. Meir, Golda, 1898-1978—Juvenile literature.
2. Prime ministers—Israel—Biography—Juvenile literature.
3. Zionists—Biography—Juvenile literature.
[1. Meir, Golda, 1898-1978. 2. Prime ministers] I. Title.
DS126.6.M42K44 1983   956.94'053'0924   [B] [92] 82-20203
ISBN 0-531-04591-9

CONTENTS

Anybody who believes in something
without reservation, believes that this
thing is right and should be, has the
stamina to meet obstacles and
overcome them. . . . From my
early youth I believed in two things:
one, the need for Jewish sovereignty,
so that Jews . . . can be master
of their own fate; and two, a society
based on justice and equality without
exploitation. But I was never so
naive or foolish as to think that if you
merely believe in something it happens.
You must struggle for it.

GOLDA MEIR

NO FIDDLER ON THE ROOF

1

No one really heard it at first. The sound was muffled and dull, as if someone were hammering on a house on the other side of town. But gradually the rhythmic beat grew louder and faster, and soon the noise became recognizable in the clear night air.

Only one child in the ragged group playing in the muddy alley stopped and listened. The others shrieked and giggled happily, absorbed in their games and mud pies. The pounding came closer, then suddenly it was upon them.

The men seemed to come out of nowhere. Fierce Cossacks, the crack horsemen of the Russian army, charged down the lane, shouting and laughing as they pulled their swords and slashed them through the air. Without slowing their gallop, they jumped their horses over the petrified bodies of the children and disappeared around the corner and into the night. Their boisterous cries of "Death to the Jews!" echoed behind them.

Shivering and sobbing, the children ran home to be comforted by mothers who were even more frightened than they, no matter how they tried to cover it with a brusque "Well, I told you not to play there!" The women knew the Cossacks' spree could easily have turned into a pogrom, a wild raid during which the soldiers, with full government approval, would ride through the streets, burning homes, looting their contents, and murdering the men, women, and children who lived there. Why? Because the people were Jewish.

Pogroms were just part of the bleak life Jews lived in Russia before the Revolution of 1917. They were Russian citizens in only two ways: they paid taxes and served in the army. Otherwise the Jewish population was confined by law to poor, small villages within a definite area along Russia's western border called the Pale of Settlement. They needed special permission to live in a city, or even to travel beyond their unpaved village lanes that were usually frozen mud in winter and swampy ooze in summer. Simple farmers or craftsmen, the Jews barely supplied their own needs. Two or three families often shared one or two dark rooms of a tiny house. They were cold, they were hungry, they were easy marks for the Cossacks, and all they could do about the situation was pray that someday things would be better.

It was into this miserable world that Golda Mabowitz was born on May 3, 1898. Because Golda's father was a skilled cabinetmaker, he had been allowed to move beyond the Pale to the city of Kiev. He lived there alone, working under a government contract to build chairs for school libraries. With the little money he made (and the promise of more), he moved his wife Bluma and daughter Sheyna from their hometown of Pinsk, and set up a small carpentry shop. Two more daughters, Golda and Zipke, were born in Kiev.

But when the contract ended, Moshe Mabowitz found it hard to make ends meet. As a carpenter with a Jewish name, when he found work at all, he was likely to receive no payment, for the Russian Christians felt no obligation to pay debts to second-class citizens. Soon Mabowitz and his family were stranded in Kiev with no money, no food, and no hope.

Rather than give up to despair, Moshe made his last dream come true. Like so many other Europeans of his time, he sold his belongings—even his tools—and bought himself a ticket to America, the Golden Land of the Russian Jews. In America anyone who worked hard got paid, no matter what his or her religion. Moshe planned to find a job and a place to live and, when he had made his fortune, to come back to Russia and give his family a new life.

He left Kiev in 1903, when Golda was five. His family, with no official permission to stay on in the city, moved back to live with Bluma's parents in Pinsk. The eldest daughter, Sheyna, spent the day at school, while the grandfather watched the two little girls. Bluma was out all day peddling her home-baked bread to Jewish housewives in the neighborhood.

Pinsk was a big town and a major center of Jewish culture. Some Jews there owned factories and businesses, providing employment for other Jews. There, too, were other Jewish children to play with, Jewish schools to go to, Jewish newspapers to read, and a synagogue to worship in. With family and friends and the promise of a better life ahead, things should have been easier for the Mabowitz women.

But there was always fighting in Golda's house. Many of the arguments were about money, because there was never enough of it. Although Bluma had soon saved enough to move out of her parents' house, the rent took all her resources. The only other possible wage-earner was four-teen-year-old Sheyna, and *she* insisted on going to school instead of working. Nothing would change her mind, and many nights Golda fell asleep to the lullaby of yelling.

Golda also heard another kind of argument in her house, a kind that could mean greater trouble for her family than poverty. This also involved Sheyna, and the friends she brought home. The argument was political, and politics was a subject best avoided. In Russia, then as now, anyone whose views differed from the government's was considered a subversive agent and was liable to arrest. People who hoped to change the government were often sent to prison in Siberia, and few returned before ten or twenty years had passed. Golda and her family lived next door to the Pinsk police station. Almost every night they heard through their thin walls the screams and cries of men and women arrested and tortured for plotting against the czar.

Sheyna exposed her family to grave danger by holding political meetings in her house, usually on Saturday mornings while her mother was at synagogue. Still in her teens, she was already a revolutionary, committed to socialism as a way of improving conditions for all Russians. She believed that when the whole community shared ownership and control of all means of production and distribution of goods, everyone would be better off, and social tensions would naturally disappear.

Sheyna's activism had another dimension. She was also dedicated to improving the lot of Russian Jews, and she dreamed of a better life, not in America, but in Palestine, the Biblical homeland of the Jewish people, now a barren strip of land on the eastern shore of the Mediterranean in a neglected corner of the declining Ottoman Empire.

Zionism, the belief that Jews should return to the homeland they had lost to the Romans in A.D. 70, was not new. Jews have included the prayer "Next Year in Jerusalem" in their Passover Seder since Roman times. But it wasn't until the late nineteenth century that the Zionist movement came into its own. In France, England, Russia—even among the Jews who had always lived in Palestine—the idea of leaving the ghettos where they'd been forced to live and returning to reclaim and rebuild the land seemed to spring up simultaneously. During the 1870s a group of European pioneers founded in Palestine a village they called Petach Tikva (Gate of Hope); a few years later a Russian group, Hovevi Zion (Lovers of Zion), joined them, determined to reestablish the Jews as a self-sufficient agricultural people after centuries of city life. Wealthy European Jews financed a farming school in Palestine and provided capital for purchasing large tracts of land for the pioneers to cultivate. Although illness and ignorance destroyed the first settlements, word of them spread through Europe, and new pioneers packed for Palestine. It finally seemed there was a way to solve the "Jewish problem." In Palestine the Jews could have their own home and no longer live as outsiders in Christian countries.

The first *aliyah* (the Hebrew word for immigration) would no doubt have proceeded slowly and steadily had it not been for the changing political climate in Europe. But anti-Semitism was becoming more open there. In Russia pogroms of new intensity terrorized the Jews. And in France the Dreyfus case exposed the prejudice rampant in what was thought to be the most enlightened of modern nations, when a Jewish officer in the French army was framed for treason.

The Dreyfus case changed the life of a Viennese journalist named Theodor Herzl. The following year, 1896, he published a modest pamphlet called *Der Judenstaat (The Jewish State)*. In it he insisted that the only way the Jews would ever be respected was by establishing their own nation, where they would have nothing and no one to fear. Herzl planned on a grander scale than did the pioneering farmers of the first *aliyah*. He wanted the Jews to do more than reclaim the land; he wanted them to form an independent, sovereign country.

Herzl publicized his dream in his newspaper column and in his special Zionist weekly called *Die Welt (The World),* and in 1897 he organized the World Zionist Congress. Representatives from Europe, America, and even Australia attended the sessions in Basle, Switzerland. All of the representatives were attired in the formal dress Herzl decreed essential to the seriousness of the occasion. And it *was* serious. For the first time in two thousand years the Jews were meeting as one nation, one people speaking with one voice. When Herzl, a striking man with a dark beard and powerful eyes, closed the congress, the enthusiasm of the delegates bordered on hysteria. He later wrote:

> If I were to sum up the Congress in one word it would be this: at Basle I founded the Jewish State. If I were to say this today, I would be greeted with universal laughter. In

*five years, perhaps, and certainly in fifty, everyone will
see it.*

Until his death in 1904, Herzl never stopped looking for a way
to secure a home in Palestine for the Jewish people. He
offered to finance Turkey's debts in return for permission for
mass Jewish immigration, and he lobbied with the world's rul-
ers for land and a legal charter. His work brought hope and
inspiration to Jews all over the world, and the second *aliyah*
began as Jews rallied to Herzl's cause.

In Russia, where a new round of bloody pogroms had
occurred, Herzl's ideas prompted the growth of another revolutionary group. The Poalei Zion (Labor Zionists) felt that the
condition of the Jews went beyond economics and czarist
repression. While sharing the socialists' goals, they also
embraced those of the Zionists and allied themselves with the
drive for nationhood and independence. This made them
doubly dangerous to the czar. It was to this group that
Golda's sister Sheyna belonged, and it was their heated discussions Golda overheard as she huddled in a corner near
the coal stove, trying to keep warm.

One night Golda heard about what had happened in the
town of Kishinev. Government agents had spread the rumor
that a Christian girl had been murdered by her Jewish
employers, and the agents encouraged the townspeople to
riot. On Easter Sunday the mob broke into Jewish homes and
shops under the very noses of the police, stealing or destroying everything they saw. By nightfall that was no longer
enough to satisfy them, and they turned on the Jews themselves with knives and sticks. Jewish children were thrown
out of windows, Jewish men and women had their eyes
gouged out or were impaled on stakes. And throughout that
terrible night and the following day, until the rioters finally collapsed from their efforts, the city officials, doctors, lawyers,
and priests did nothing to stop the mayhem. The police inter-
vened only once—to disarm a group of Jews who were trying
to defend themselves with broken branches.

Golda listened to the story in horror. She saw in her mind little children like herself bleeding on the muddy streets, crying for their dead mothers. She remembered, too, something that had happened when she was much younger, perhaps three or four. It was just getting dark, and her father had come into their little house in Kiev with some boards and nails. With the help of the man who lived upstairs, he started hammering the wood over the doors and windows. From her seat on the stairs Golda heard the word "pogrom" and, without knowing what it meant, understood that something dreadful might happen to her family. Now, hearing about the Jews of Kishinev, she wondered what good those boards would have done.

At that moment, perhaps, Golda became a Zionist. Even though she was only a child, she realized that because she was Jewish she would always be an outsider living in fear of a break in the uneasy truce between herself and her neighbors. Suddenly Sheyna's dream of freedom and equality in a Jewish nation made sense. Only when the Jews were a majority in their own land could they live in peace and dignity and protect their children from the horrors of Kishinev.

Sheyna influenced Golda in other ways besides politically. With Bluma gone most of the day, Sheyna became a surrogate mother, telling Golda stories and singing songs and, later on, teaching her to read and write and do arithmetic. Beyond these skills, however, Sheyna gave Golda a philosophy for living. Always a perfectionist, Sheyna believed there was only one way to do anything—the right way—and that you therefore had to lead your life according to the highest principles. She taught Golda by her example that it wasn't enough to believe in a cause. You had to make things happen, struggle to overcome the obstacles with all your might, for thought is nothing without action. Golda later wrote of her sister: "She was a shining example, my dearest friend and my mentor. Even late in life, when we were both grown women, grandmothers, in fact, Sheyna was the one person whose praise and approval . . . meant the most to me. Sheyna, in fact, is part and parcel of the story of my life."

Golda's early childhood was overshadowed by fear, hunger, and poverty, but there were sweet times as well. After her mother found lodging over a bakery for her family, the girl no longer dreaded the cold, for the ovens warmed them all night long. And Golda played with other children and looked forward to the Jewish holidays and Sabbaths, when the whole family—aunts, uncles, grandparents, and cousins—would gather around the table, drinking tea and talking well into the night.

Moshe Mabowitz spent three years alone in America while his family waited in Pinsk for his return. Unable to find suitable work in New York, he had moved west until he reached Milwaukee. That city was growing fast and offered lots of work for a carpenter. Many other European immigrants had also found their way there, so the atmosphere was not totally alien to him. By 1905 he had a good job with the railroad, and he decided to stay. He wrote his family that soon he would have enough money to buy their passage to this wonderful new country.

What a relief this was to Bluma! No longer would she have to be the sole support of her family, working day and night to keep a roof over their heads. No longer would she have to see her daughters go hungry. Most important, once they left Russia, no longer would she have to worry that the police would raid one of Sheyna's ever more frequent meetings and ship her—and her innocent family—off to Siberia. They were going to the land of milk and honey, of freedom and equality—America.

The Mabowitzes began getting ready for their journey even before Moshe sent their ticket money. They had to, for going to America in 1906 was about as easy as going to the moon. Once you got there, you couldn't come back. Emigrating meant saying good-bye to all your relatives and playmates, and to the only home, language, and customs you had ever known. It meant a long journey overland to a seaport in Europe, and then a longer ocean voyage, usually spent on the deck of a ship or in the hold, for who could afford the luxury of a cabin?

For Bluma, traveling with three young girls, two of whom were under the age of eight, the trip was especially hard. On the day they had to leave Pinsk, they put on all the clothes they could manage and carried the rest of their possessions to the railway station in a few boxes and bundles. There on the platform next to the steaming train, Golda hugged her grandfather for the last time.

They were leaving Russia illegally. There hadn't been enough time or money for proper passports, so the Mabowitzes used the papers of people who had died. These "new" identities didn't quite fit. Bluma was supposed to be a young woman of twenty, and eighteen-year-old Sheyna had to look twelve. Golda became five years old again, while little Zipke had to travel with a childless stranger who nevertheless had a passport for a little girl. The emigrants quickly realized that the officials wouldn't notice the discrepancies if they were paid enough, and so at each stop of the train Bluma pulled out another of the coins she had sewn into her garments. In the end it was the bribery and not the false papers that got them through the border check and into Poland.

Here they were to meet the train for Belgium. With all the other passengers they crowded into an unheated shack where there was nothing to sit on but a few dirty blankets spread on the earthen floor. It was here that Bluma discovered that all their luggage had been stolen. Left with little more than the clothes they wore, the Mabowitzes waited for two days until the connecting train came. Golda tried to keep Zipke from crying by singing to her and telling her exciting stories about the wonders of America.

After a two-day trip across Europe, sitting upright on hard wooden seats clutching the few belongings they had left, Bluma and her daughters arrived in Antwerp. Here they waited again, this time for a ship to take them across the Atlantic. They stayed in an immigration home, a sort of hotel for frightened and weary travelers. Here they had their first hot meal and bath since leaving Pinsk the week before. During breakfast on their second day at the home, Bluma heard their name called for the medical examination. Although it was instituted to keep all travelers healthy, this was a dreaded procedure, for even so small a problem as head lice could get you sent all the way back home. But the Mabowitzes all passed and later that day were told to get their bundles and board a ship for Québec, Canada.

The last and most uncomfortable stage of the journey had begun. Steerage passengers were jammed eight to a dark stuffy room at the bottom of the ship, too low for a porthole, but just the right height to make sure the voyagers felt every roll, pitch, and heave of the vessel as it plowed through the stormy northern seas. The bunks were tiny and without bedding or blankets. There was no dining room, either. If you wanted to eat, you stood outside your cabin with a tin plate and cup, and a sailor would slop out some watery gruel or thin soup from a bucket he carried as he walked by.

Her family was seasick for most of the two-week voyage, but Golda felt fine. She spent long hours on deck, staring at the sea, trying to imagine what Milwaukee would be like. Or she and the other children on board would run and play and swap stories about the unlimited riches and opportunities waiting for them in the Goldene Medina (the Golden Land). How else could they tame their fear and worry about being strangers in a strange new land?

Another train took them from Québec to Milwaukee. It had been a month of constant travel since she had kissed her grandfather good-bye, and Golda, too exhausted to watch America slip past the windows, was sound asleep when the train stopped for the last time. Quickly and anxiously Bluma roused her, then gathered her daughters and their few bags, and herded them off the train.

Once on the platform they stopped. Now what? Passengers, porters, and peddlars surrounded them, jabbering in a mysterious tongue. They had reached their destination, but no familiar face was there to greet them.

The station emptied. The Mabowitzes were left alone by the track, except for a tall man who was walking slowly down the length of the train, peering into every window.

Bluma recognized him first. To Golda and Zipke, too young to really remember him, their mother's tears meant only two things: that this handsome stranger was their father, and that now they were going to be a real family again.

THE
NEW LAND

2

Imagine waking up in a world in which all your hopes and dreams had come true.

That's how Golda felt when she opened her eyes the next morning and looked around the tiny room her father had brought them to. The place was warm and clean, their bellies were still full from last night's supper, and they were all together again. Who could ask for more?

Moshe Mabowitz could. The sight of his family huddled on the railway platform in their dark, shapeless dresses, kerchiefs on their heads, and ragged bundles at their feet was too strong a reminder of the hard times in the old country. After three years he was already an American. He had shaved off his beard, made friends, and joined both a synagogue and a trade union. These foreign-looking females didn't fit into his new life. But he had a solution ready.

Right after breakfast on their second day in Milwaukee, Moshe piloted his family onto a streetcar. No one said much as they rode over the wide, paved streets and tried to decipher the signs printed in an unfamiliar alphabet. Everywhere was noise and activity. The streetcar shared the roadway with horses and carriages, cars and bicycles. Men and women in summer finery strolled along the sidewalks, stopping every now and then to peek into a glittering shop window. Golda stared in amazement at a little girl of about her own age who proudly pushed an elaborate wicker doll carriage in which a blue-eyed china doll reclined against white eyelet pillows. Even Golda's nose was astonished by all the new smells of America.

Once downtown, Moshe pulled them off the trolley and pushed them through the doors of Schuster's Department Store. Here was another marvel; who in Pinsk had ever been in a five-story skyscraper? Or seen a shop with such an array of hats, shoes, blouses, gloves, and even umbrellas under one roof? Fortunately Moshe knew exactly what he wanted for his girls, and so they were spared the exquisite agony of having to choose among all the pretty new things. Golda, Zipke, and Bluma were delighted with their American clothes and, even more, with the ice cream sundaes they ate to celebrate the day.

Only Sheyna remained quiet and serious during the shopping expedition. Afraid that if she changed herself on the outside, she might change on the inside, too, she rejected her father's gifts and kept her old black dress. The clash of her stubbornness and her father's disappointment created much tension in the Mabowitz household for many months.

Within weeks of their arrival Bluma found larger quarters for her family on Walnut Street. Their neighbors were other poor Jewish immigrants who, like themselves, spoke very little English. Their common language was Yiddish, a mixture of Hebrew and various German dialects, which was spoken by almost all the Ashkenazim, or Northern European Jews. Bound by a common culture and religion, the immigrants helped one another adapt to America in these voluntary ghettos.

The new apartment seemed palatial to Golda. It filled the entire first floor of a big wooden house with a porch that was planted squarely on a small weed-filled lot. The Mabowitzes lived in two rooms and a tiny kitchenette. Bluma and Moshe slept in the front room that doubled as a parlor; the girls, quite using to sharing beds, moved into the back room. There was no electricity, but the gaslights that lit the rooms were a lot cleaner and less smelly than the oil lamps of Pinsk. And the apartment came with two miracles. One was the water that rushed out of a tap into the kitchen sink with the turn of a knob; no more pumping an old well outside on a freezing winter night. The other wonder was in a small shed in the backyard. While the apartment had no bathroom, it did have a flush toilet in the outhouse, and it was several weeks before anyone stopped giving the chain an extra pull just for the fun of seeing the water gurgle down the drain.

But for Bluma the real attraction of the apartment lay in a third room with a big window facing the street. This, she decided, was an excellent location for a shop. The family had scarcely settled in when she opened her dairy and grocery store, despite the fact that she knew no English, had no experience in retailing, and didn't have any idea of what to stock her shelves with. Luckily her neighbors rallied to her aid, and those who had been in America longest taught her a few English words, showed her how to behave like a shopkeeper, explained how to operate the cash register and scales, and, most important, let her know which of her potential customers were good credit risks. The store belonged to Bluma alone. It was she who borrowed money to buy her stock, it was she who weighed the oranges and wrapped the cheese, and it was she who got up at dawn to go to the wholesale market and drag the day's purchases home behind her.

Her family wanted no part in this venture. Her husband, interpreting her enterprise as a silent criticism of his ability to support them, grudgingly built her a few shelves and vowed that was the last time he would set foot in the store. Sheyna characteristically refused to have anything to do with this capitalist venture. "I did not come to America to turn into a shopkeeper, a social parasite," she declared grandly, and went off to sew buttonholes in a tailor shop instead. Zipke was too young to be much use. That left the unwilling Golda to mind the store whenever her mother went out.

Golda was really the best choice for the job. By the end of that first summer she seemed to be the most Americanized of all the Mabowitzes. On her own she had picked up enough English to make herself understood outside the neighborhood, and she could now make her way about the city independently. She embraced her new country wholeheartedly, seeing every day as a new adventure. The greatest thrill of those first months, however, came in early September, when Golda watched her father march with his union in Milwaukee's Labor Day parade.

Golda had led her family to the street corner her father had said afforded the best view. Dressed in their best clothes, pressed in next to ice cream vendors, flag wavers, women with big hats, and men with small children on their shoulders, they glanced up and down the street wondering what would happen next. None of them could have told you exactly what a parade was, but they were very excited nonetheless. When the marchers finally reached them and Golda saw her father in his good suit striding along with his fellow carpenters, she was ecstatic. This was what American freedom meant. As she wrote later: "To see my father marching on that September day was like coming out of the dark into the light."

Her little sister Zipke had quite a different reaction. When she saw the mounted police leading the parade, she began screaming, "The Cossacks! The Cossacks are coming!" and had to be taken home and put to bed. The sunlight of America had not entirely dispelled the Russian shadows. Even though Golda patiently explained that the police were escorting the marchers, not routing them, Zipke remained inconsolable.

September brought another joy to Golda's life; she started school. Because she was eight years old, Golda entered as a second grader, and she loved it all from the first day. She was bright enough to rise quickly to the top of her class, and popular enough to make many friends. In fact, two of the girls in that class stayed Golda's lifelong friends.

Now it was more torture than ever for Golda to have to watch the store in the morning, for that made her late for school. She couldn't make her mother understand that each time she was tardy she suffered not only embarrassment but a demerit as well. But Bluma wouldn't believe that education was important. In Russia girls never went to school. Why should it be different here? Not until a truant officer explained to Bluma that when she kept her daughter out of school she was breaking the law could Golda count on slipping into her seat before the late bell.

Golda learned more than fractions at the Fourth Street School. She learned how she was going to live. During her years there she decided that what was important was to be honest with herself and her friends and to get involved in causes that benefited others, not just herself. By 1909 her social conscience was already alive and at work. That year, when she was an eleven-year-old fourth grader, Golda organized what she called her first "public work."

In those days, even though school was free, the textbooks were not. Many children in Golda's school were too poor to pay for even the most battered books. Golda, aching for their mortification when they had to explain why they had no books, and burning at this inequality in the "free public school" system, convinced a few of her girl friends to help her do something about it.

Calling themselves the American Young Sisters Society (because they all had sisters), the girls launched a book fund. First they collected door-to-door. Golda soon developed a technique for dealing with reluctant givers. The young girl would look them straight in the eye, say "I wasn't born among royalty either," and walk away with a donation.

The Young Sisters' major project was a "public meeting and entertainment." Golda rented an auditorium (and for the rest of her life marveled that anyone would rent anything to an eleven-year-old) and placed advertisements in the paper, promising to pay for them later. The others painted posters, sent invitations to everyone in the school district, and, in their spare time, rehearsed their poems and songs for the entertainment.

To their amazement dozens of people came to the Saturday night meeting, many just out of curiosity to see what fourth graders could do. The high point of the evening was Golda's speech. Without notes or rehearsal, the young girl gave the first of what would be scores of "speeches from my head." In simple, heartfelt words she explained that all children needed books, not just those who could afford them. Her talk opened purses throughout the hall; the girls collected more money than they thought possible; and, best of all, a Milwaukee newspaper covered the meeting and gave the cause extra publicity.

How proud Golda was! How pleased with her work! Her only disappointment was that Sheyna had not been there to see it. But her older sister had gone to be cured of tuberculosis at the Jewish Hospital for Consumptives in Denver. Her boyfriend, Sam Korngold, had followed her there, and soon they were married and the happy parents of a daughter.

Life was easier in the Mabowitz house without Sheyna's iron will. While they were never well off (neither the carpentry nor the grocery ever showed a profit), their life was rich in other ways. Not terribly observant Jews, they nevertheless celebrated and preserved Jewish culture and tradition. Golda grew up in a kosher household. A Yiddish newspaper came home in her father's pocket every night, and Yiddish books lined their shelves. The girls were sent briefly to a Talmud Torah (religious school) where they learned a smattering of Hebrew, the language of the scriptures. The Mabowitzes were also interested in the larger world. "The house was always alive with public affairs," recalled Golda, and with culture, too, as visiting Yiddish lecturers and intellectuals were often put up for the night on the sofa in the front room. Both her parents also devoted time and energy to Jewish aid societies like B'nai B'rith and the American Jewish Congress, sharing what little they had with those who had even less.

Golda Mabowitz (at far right, wearing a white dress) graduated at the top of her grammar school class in 1910.

Moshe and Bluma seemed to have adapted to American ways very well, but actually they held on to many Old World beliefs and values. Golda, who had jumped into the New World with both feet, found as she grew older that her values conflicted with her parents'. Soon angry shouts and stormy silences filled the apartment again. Why? Golda wanted to go to high school and college; she dreamed of becoming a teacher. Her parents, still not convinced that a girl needed any education at all, insisted she leave school after eighth grade and work in her mother's store. They became even more adamant about this when they discovered that teachers were frequently forbidden to marry. "Why study to be an old maid?" Bluma asked repeatedly. Marriage and motherhood were the only two occupations she understood.

Rather than work in the shop, Golda took a job wrapping packages at a downtown department store even before she graduated at the top of her grammar school class. The job didn't pay much, but Golda soon earned enough money to buy herself a new winter coat and a few feelings of independence. In the fall she started high school anyway, and an uneasy peace reigned at home. But when Bluma arranged a marriage for her with a nice, respectable, middle-aged man named Goodstein, the fourteen-year-old Golda knew another war was imminent. That night she wrote a long and angry letter to Sheyna, begging for advice.

Almost by return mail came the reply:

> No, you shouldn't stop school. You are too young to work; you have a good chance to become something. . . . My advice is you should get ready and come to us. We are not rich either, but you will have good chances here to study and we will do all we can for you. . . . First, you'll have all the opportunities to study; second, you'll have plenty to eat; third, you'll have all the necessary clothes a person ought to have. . . .

This was all the encouragement Golda needed. Knowing that her parents would never give her permission to go to Denver, she began to plan her escape. Now she saved her wages for her train ticket and augmented the small sum by giving English lessons to recent immigrants. Her best friend Regina agreed to stash Golda's suitcase so that when it was time to go, Golda could slip out of the house without attracting any attention.

The night before she left, an anxious and unhappy Golda wrote a note explaining her actions. Sheyna's advice echoed in her head: "The main thing is never to be excited. Always be calm and act cool. This way of action will always bring you good results. Be brave."

Golda walked out of the house the next morning as if she were going off to school. Instead she headed for the railroad station and the Denver Express. Her sophistication did not extend so far, however, as to know that trains ran according to schedules, and that hers wouldn't arrive before noon. So while Golda's family was reading her note, and yelling and crying and trying to get Regina to tell them what was going on, Golda herself was sitting on her suitcase at the station, becoming more convinced with every passing minute that her parents would appear and drag her home by her long dark braid. But the train came before they did, and the next day Golda was drinking tea with Sheyna and Sam and telling them her adventures. It wasn't until the following week that she found out about the scene at home that morning. Regina wrote to tell her that everyone in Milwaukee was sure Golda hadn't gone to Denver at all, but had eloped with an Italian!

Once the break had been made, Golda found it easier to communicate with her mother. Her schedule didn't leave much time for letter-writing, however. After school Golda helped Sam in his dry-cleaning store, then went home to study and help Sheyna with dinner. Nor was there much time in the evening, for the Korngold apartment was a gathering place for other Russian Jews who had come for treatment at the consumptive hospital. In the group were socialists, anarchists, and Zionists; most of them were bachelors. Their free-wheeling and passionate discussions lasted well into the night. Much of the talk was over Golda's head, but some of

what she heard influenced her life and convictions more than anything she could have learned in high school.

Golda soon found she was paying closest attention to the Social Zionists among Sheyna's guests. She had long been sympathetic to the Zionist dream of a Jewish homeland, "a place where no one would be in want or be exploited or live in fear of other men." But now she was equally sympathetic to their socialist views, their commitment to the building of this land and its just society through the physical labor of each and every individual.

From these ardent young men Golda heard about the pioneers in Palestine. Another great *aliyah* was under way: young people were leaving their wealthy, cultured, and comfortable homes in Europe for tents pitched on Palestine's arid soil. The few settlements started during the first *aliyah* were not enough; at that rate Jews would always be a minority in Palestine. This more forceful generation wouldn't wait for the national charter that Herzl and the first Zionists thought was so important. As one of them, David Ben-Gurion, put it, "The way for Jews to reclaim their ancient land is not by argument, or by listing historical precedents, but by *labor*. By creating something fruitful where previously there was nothing."

And nothing was there. The rich Turkish and Arab landowners were quick to see just how much these *chalutzim* (pioneers) wanted their land, and obligingly sold them vast tracts of the very worst of it. Here the *chalutzim* founded the farming communes—the kibbutzim—that symbolized their ideals. In a kibbutz each member contributed labor and talent to the good of the group and received from it no more than he or she needed, making it a truly egalitarian organization. Life here was hard; the labor exhausting; pestilence and fever

While living in Denver
with her sister, Sheyna,
Golda was photographed
with the Korngold family.

daily companions. But all was tolerable when endured for the great dream of Jewish statehood.

Golda was fascinated by these stories about Palestine, and she daydreamed of the time when she could add her labor to that of these hardy pioneers. She also dreamed about one of Sheyna's less articulate guests, a shy, bespectacled young sign painter named Morris Myerson. Morris was different from the other visitors in that he was entirely self-educated, and his personal curriculum had taken him through literature, art, and music instead of politics and economics. Golda had never met anyone like him before, and soon she had a second pile of books beside her bed, books Morris had recommended. For the first time in her life Golda was reading poetry.

Golda's large bown eyes and thick wavy hair had already attracted a lot of suitors, but she chose to spend almost every evening with Morris. On weekends he took her to free concerts in the park, carefully explaining the symphonies they were hearing. Golda paid as much attention to this private music appreciation course as she could, but, she later confessed, most of her was paying attention to whether her dress looked neat or whether the dye in her new red straw hat would run all over her face if that threatening cloud decided to burst.

Sheyna quickly noticed her young sister's busy social life. Now more mother than revolutionary, she tried to forbid both Golda's participation in the evening debates and her friendship with Morris. If Golda had come to Denver to study, then that's all she should do. Besides, the neighbors were talking about how much Golda was out, and Sheyna wanted no part in any scandal. Soon the Korngold home was as war-torn as the Mabowitzes'. Late one night, after a particularly bitter dispute, Golda moved out, taking with her only the clothes she was wearing. Fortunately she had friends to take her in, for only as she heard the door slam behind her did Golda stop and think about where she would go.

It was several months before the two stubborn sisters made up after their quarrel, but, in the meantime, Golda found a job and her own room, and had a wonderful time being sixteen and independent. When her parents learned about her actions, though, they begged her to come home, promising that she could not only finish high school but train to be a teacher at the Milwaukee Normal School.

A much more self-possessed and sophisticated Golda returned to the house on Walnut Street. She'd blossomed in Denver, and most of the roses in her cheeks were from Morris. Although he had to stay behind and care for his sister, he had sworn his love for Golda. The two agreed to write every day until he could join her in Milwaukee and marry her. Golda was, as she admitted to Regina, "in a blissful state of mind." This postal romance did not proceed smoothly, however. Bluma was intensely curious about the daily envelope from Denver, and she quietly had the letters translated into Yiddish for her. A furious Golda promptly advised Morris to direct his letters to Regina's house instead.

Golda also brought her political commitment back with her. "Slowly, Zionism was beginning to fill my mind and my life," she recalled. In Milwaukee the pioneering stories she'd heard in Denver were brought to life by the Palestinians themselves. These visitors spoke about the fledgling kibbutzim and the new town of Tel Aviv, the first Jewish city to be built in almost two thousand years. Their descriptions of how all Palestinians, men and women, worked together as equals, sharing hardship and danger and pride, fascinated Golda, and she went to hear them at every opportunity.

And she had many chances. These Palestinian speakers were not in America on pleasure trips. They were here to find help for the *yishuv* (the Jewish community in Palestine), which was caught in the Middle Eastern front of World War I. The Jews wanted to form their own fighting unit, as a way of both liberating the country and strengthening the Jewish claim to it, and *yishuv* leaders traveled to the United States to find recruits from among the thousands of immigrants who were still not eligible to serve in the United States Army. They spoke so glowingly and convincingly because they needed more Jews to help them in the homeland. Golda was enthralled by the idea, and she volunteered. She was disappointed to discover, however, that equality had not been carried that far; women would still have to serve another way.

Another cause claimed her attention at this time. The European Jews, victims of the "war to end all wars," were being shot, beaten, or forced to leave their homes by advancing armies. Golda saw the money, food, and clothing she sent as merely a short-term measure. Her people needed a home of their own. How could Golda enjoy her freedom until all Jews were free?

But she refused to join the Labor Zionist party until she was sure she could move to Palestine. She would not talk if she could not act; she would not tell others to emigrate while she stayed comfortably in Milwaukee.

One of the reasons for her hesitation was her age. She was barely seventeen, still in school, with a future of unlimited opportunity opening before her. The other reason was Morris. In their letters they tried to plan their life together, but in between the tender words and gallant compliments a very serious problem appeared. Morris did not share Golda's fervent Zionism. In one letter he wrote:

> I don't know whether to be glad or sorry that you seem to be so enthusiastic a nationalist. I am altogether passive in this matter, though I give you full credit for your activity, as I do all others engaged in doing something toward helping a distressed nation. . . . But . . . I do not care particularly as to whether the Jews are going to suffer in Russia or in the Holy Land.

Golda ignored his warning and became more and more involved in the Zionist cause. She organized meetings and seminars and sponsored relief drives and parades for Jewish war victims. To her parents' dismay she took to making speeches on street corners, something no respectable girl did. Moshe was so enraged at this activity that one night he threatened to come after her and pull her off her soapbox by her hair. Golda, too stubborn to give in to such talk, went to her rally anyway and spoke so eloquently that her father forgot all about bringing her home. All he could say to his wife when he walked in the house alone was "I don't know where she gets it from." Golda always considered that speech the most successful one she ever made.

When she wasn't at rallies, Golda was teaching, not at the kind of school she was being trained for, but at a Yiddish *folkschule*. A few afternoons each week she taught the Jewish children of Milwaukee the language and literature that united most of European Jewry. By acquainting them with their heritage, Golda felt she was preparing them for a life in the homeland.

Then, shortly before her eighteenth birthday, Golda formally joined the Poalei Zion (Labor Zionist party) and took her first real steps toward Palestine. She couldn't persuade Morris to go with her, however. He now viewed their disagreement over the Palestinian question as a symptom of other, greater personal differences between them. They decided to stop seeing each other, but that made them even more miserable. Golda buried her unhappiness and anxiety in her work for the party. "There was always something," she wrote, "that took precedence over my private worries and therefore served to distract me from them—a situation that was not to change much in the course of the next six decades."

In November 1917, Golda got both Morris and Palestine. That month, when it looked as if the Allies would win the war and the Ottoman Empire would surrender Palestine to the British, Lord Arthur Balfour, Britain's foreign secretary, sent a letter to Lord Rothschild, a prominent supporter of the Jewish homeland since before Herzl. It read in part: "His Majesty's Governments views with favour the establishment in Palestine of a national home for the Jewish people, and will use their best endeavours to facilitate the achievement of this object. . . ."

Not that the British intended to do anything about establishing a homeland right away. Jews would have to settle and stay in Palestine for many years. They'd have to build their own hospitals and schools, farms and factories. They'd have to establish their own unofficial government and prove that they could function as a nation by themselves. Only then would the British relinquish control and let the Jewish nation be born. But the Balfour Declaration marked the first time an important country had ever agreed to the creation of a Jewish state, and Jews everywhere rejoiced.

Many now resolved to go to Palestine, and one of them was Morris. There was now no reason for the couple not to marry. On December 24, 1917, Morris and Golda stood together under the traditional bridal canopy and exchanged vows (one of which was to go to Palestine) before a rabbi. This was one fight Golda's parents won. Golda and Morris had wanted a civil ceremony with no guests and no party. Why should they, modern socialists as they were, be bound by ancient rites? But Bluma insisted that such a wedding would kill her and disgrace the family. The bride and groom discussed the problem at length and finally decided that a religious ritual wouldn't compromise their principles—and Bluma got the party she wanted.

The two Myersons set up housekeeping in a small apartment of their own, but Golda wasn't there much. She'd left college when she realized that a Wisconsin teaching certificate wouldn't be much use in the Palestinian hinterland, and she was now working for Poalei Zion. Because she was young, attractive, and fluent in English and Yiddish, Golda was one of their most popular speakers, and she traveled all over the country organizing new Zionist groups and raising money. For this she was paid fifteen dollars a week plus expenses, although she paid for her frequent ice cream binges out of her own pocket. Neither the travel nor the low wages troubled her, for she was working for her cause.

Golda and Morris Myerson at the time of their wedding in 1917

Her parents, however, were shocked that a bride would leave her husband and go on the road. But Morris understood that Golda wouldn't say no to the party. During her absences he worked, read, and fixed up the apartment, and he always had fresh flowers waiting for her when she came back from a trip. If he resented his enforced solitude, he never complained. Besides, it pleased him that Golda was so happy.

Why shouldn't she be? She had a satisfying job, a husband she loved, and every week she added a few more dollars to her "Palestine bank account." Sheyna, however, warned her that she was paying too much attention to public affairs and not enough to private ones. "As far as personal happiness is concerned, grasp it, Goldie, hold it tight," she wrote. "You behold happiness without much effort and don't grasp the real value of it."

But Golda knew only that she had her cake and was enjoying every bite. Far too involved in her political life, she did not see the hurt in Morris's eyes each time she reached for her battered suitcase. As she eagerly packed fo her next trip, she blithely assured her husband that once they got to Palestine she wouldn't have to travel, and *then* they could be together.

THE PIONEER

3

Once again Golda was getting ready to cross the sea to a new home and a new life.

She, Morris, and the twenty friends who had decided to join her on the adventure emptied out their Palestine bank accounts and purchased tickets for the S.S. *Pocahontas*. The band of pioneers then got rid of all the things they felt they wouldn't need in Palestine. Away went tables and chairs, curtains, irons, and winter coats; they were all sure they'd be camping in tents in a very mild climate. Golda and Morris decided to keep their hand-cranked phonograph and records so they could at least have music in the wilderness, and they stocked up on thick wool blankets so that they'd be comfortable sleeping on the ground.

In the early spring of 1921 they were all set. Only the farewell visits remained. Golda parted tearfully from her parents in Milwaukee and made a last stop in Chicago where Sheyna, Sam, and their two children were living. Golda knew her sister really didn't approve of this traipsing off to Palestine. "Don't you think," Sheyna had replied to one of Golda's enthusiastic letters, "that there's a middle road for idealism, right here on the spot?"

But now, in Sheyna's tiny living room, something had changed. Sheyna listened so intently to Golda's talk of passages, provisions, and pioneers that at one point Sam jokingly asked her, "Maybe you'd like to go too?"

He later called this question his big mistake, for at once Sheyna looked up and said, "Yes!" Seizing the chance to put her long-dormant Zionist principles into action, in the shocked silence that followed she asked Sam to stay in Chicago and send her the money she and the children would need to get settled in the Holy Land. Then he could emigrate too. While Sam tried desperately to change her mind, Sheyna calmly packed the children's clothes, kissed him good-bye, and left to meet the ship in New York.

The excited group boarded the *Pocahontas* and set out to sea on May 23, 1921, confident of reaching Palestine in two weeks' time. But the story of their journey reads like a script for a cliff-hanging movie serial. Anything that could go wrong, did—and right from the start. Believing the ship to be totally unseaworthy, the crew mutinied the first day out, mixing seawater with the drinking water, adding salt to the provisions, and "fixing" the engines so that the vessel listed and stopped at irregular intervals. What should have been a two-day sail to pick up more passengers in Boston took nine days, and three of Golda's party, an elderly couple and a young bride, understandably ended their voyage there.

Despite a new crew and repaired engines, the trip across the Atlantic was even worse than the one up the American coast. Sabotage began again as soon as they reached the open sea. Pumps, boilers, and condensers broke down. Passengers dined on pickled beef, salty rice, and brackish water. Mysterious fires erupted in the hold; broken portholes flooded cabins and storerooms; and crewmen filled the makeshift brig.

The *Pocahontas* had to dock in the Azores for another unscheduled week of repairs. The voyage had already lasted one month. Before it ended, one hapless passenger broke her leg, and another died. The captain's brother went mad and had to be chained and locked in his cabin, where he cried and screamed loudly all day. Finally the captain, facing arrest for proceeding with so mutinous a crew, apparently committed suicide by jumping overboard. But when his body was recovered, it was found that his hands had been tied together and then to a lead pipe, something a suicide was not likely to have managed.

With a great sense of relief the pioneers disembarked in Naples, Italy. They spent the next five days reassuring family and friends that they had not gone down with the ship, replenishing their supplies, and trying to find a way to go on to Palestine, for no steamship company would sell them tickets. Inspired by the Arab riots that had rocked Palestine earlier that spring, the Arab ferrymen who took travelers across Jaffa's shallow harbor to the shore were threatening to throw all Jewish passengers into the sea.

The only route left was by ship to Egypt and then by rail to Palestine. But as Golda's pioneers stood on the pier, ready to sail for Alexandria, they found that a fresh disaster had struck. All their luggage had disappeared en route to the dock, and they had to board the waiting vessel with only the steamship company's assurance that their belongings would be sent on to them once they were found.

A second cloud shadowed this part of the trip. Also on board was a group of sturdy Lithuanian *chalutzim* who were quite contemptuous of the "soft Americans" and refused to speak to them. To prove their earnestness and gumption, Golda convinced her friends to give up their cabins and dining room meals to sleep and eat on deck, just as the Lithuanians did. The gesture did little to improve relations between the two parties, but added much to the discomfort of the trip. Yet because Golda was sure it was the right thing to do, her companions willingly followed her lead.

From Alexandria they continued by train through Egypt's Sinai Peninsula to Tel Aviv. Everywhere they were surrounded by sand. They had no water, and at every stop ragged, fly-ridden beggars pressed around them. Above all there was an unbreathable heat. Only by concentrating on how each jolt of the filthy train carried them closer to the end of their journey, and by singing brave songs about the return to Zion, could Golda keep her comrades from becoming utterly despondent.

And when, on July 14, the weary pilgrims finally stepped off the train in the Holy Land, Golda realized that her task would be even harder than she had foreseen. Before them lay the city of Tel Aviv, the "hill of spring." What a cruel joke *that* was. From the bare platform on which they stood, uncertain of what to do next, all they could see in any direction was deep sand and one or two small stucco houses, blazing white in the noonday sun.

"Well, Golda, here we are. Now we can go home!"

Golda did not smile at her friend's quip.

They spent their first night in Palestine at Tel Aviv's only hotel and, to their horror, shared their mattresses with bedbugs. Morris's shiny American razor disappeared during the night. And in the morning they learned that the people they had come to stay with were giving up and returning to New York the very next day.

Dispirited, confused, and remorseful about dragging her friends along on so grim an adventure, Golda began to doubt that she really was cut out for the life of a pioneer. Repelled by the sour milk and spoiled meat, the only food she could afford in the markets, frustrated by the flies that swarmed everywhere, she wondered how she could live in the wilderness.

She was even more discouraged to learn that she and Morris couldn't simply go to a kibbutz and set to work, but would have to apply for formal admission to one in the fall. Faced with an unexpected summer in Tel Aviv, the Myersons, the Korngolds, and two others found a cheap, roomy apartment with no electricity and a common bathroom in the courtyard. Sheyna kept house while the others took any jobs they could find in order to meet the rent. Golda gave private English lessons and practiced her Hebrew, the "new" language of Palestine, while waiting for an answer from the kibbutz.

They had chosen to apply to the kibbutz at Merhavia because of friends' recommendations, but the members there turned down the Myersons' first application. They were sure the Americans were spoiled and too weak to do heavy labor. Nor did they want married couples; the settlement couldn't yet afford the "luxury" of babies. Most surprisingly, the kibbutzniks doubted Golda's commitment. They saw her teaching as too intellectual an occupation for a would-be pioneer. It would have been better if she'd washed floors instead!

The Myersons promptly reapplied, and this time they were accepted. Leaving their companions, who had elected to build the homeland in the relative comfort of the city, they arrived at Merhavia in the late fall of 1921. The kibbutz was just a cluster of small buildings and spindly trees on the swampy Plain of Jezreel (now called the Emek). Golda and Morris were put to work at once.

Since on a kibbutz the jobs are rotated among the members, everyone has a turn at everything. The first jobs the Myersons got were the hardest Merhavia had to offer. Golda was given a straw basket and sent to the almond grove with instructions to pick a basketful each hour; Morris was sent to pick stones out of a rocky hillside so that the land could be plowed. When they returned to their room that first night, they could barely move, but they knew that if they failed to show up for dinner, their comrades would shake their heads and mutter, "What did we say? Those are Americans for you!"

From the almond grove Golda moved into the barley fields, tree nurseries, and hen houses. Despite her deep-seated dislike of chickens, Golda attended an intensive course in poultry management and soon made Merhavia's fowl yard a model of efficiency for other kibbutzim, as well as a source of fresh eggs for the table.

But it was kitchen duty she most enjoyed, although this was the least popular job in the community. The women kibbutzniks, eager to prove their ability to do men's work, resisted traditional women's tasks. "Why is it so much better to work in the barn and feed cows, rather than in the kitchen and

feed your comrades?'' Golda often asked. No one ever had a good answer for her.

Golda wanted to work in the kitchen mainly because the food was so awful. Their diet was based on sour grains cooked in bitter oil to an unpleasant mush, canned corned beef, a few homegrown vegetables, and herring in tomato sauce. Quinine tablets to ward off malarial chills were served with every meal. During Golda's first tour in the kitchen she changed the menu. Instead of the usual herring for breakfast, she served the astonished kibbutzniks oatmeal before they went out into the fields. "Baby food!" they complained—as they cleaned their bowls.

Golda also surprised the other kibbutzniks by spreading tablecloths for special Sabbath meals. She always ironed her dresses, drab and shapeless as they were, and wore stockings in the evening. Even Morris shocked his comrades when he painted floral designs on the dingy white walls of their room. Their fellow kibbutzniks frowned on this middle-class American behavior. But no one ever objected to the Myersons' phonograph and collection of scratchy records. In fact, Golda always suspected that the phonograph was what had clinched their admission to Merhavia.

Despite the physical exhaustion, the malaria and sandfly fever, despite the swarming gnats, flies, and mosquitoes that plagued her whenever she went outdoors, despite even the constant threat of Arab attack, Golda thrived on this life she'd always dreamed of. In the summer she'd be out with the others at four o'clock in the morning and back from the fields before the arrival of the terrible noon sun. She slogged through cold, wet mud, the likes of which she hadn't seen

*On the kibbutz
at Merhavia, Golda
overcame her aversion
to chickens and became
an expert on poultry.*

since she left Pinsk, to feed the chickens in the winter. After supper she was the life of the kibbutz parties, always ready to sing and dance into the night. And many times Golda would still be in the kitchen in the early hours of the morning, fixing snacks for the men who were just coming off guard duty.

So vital a personality was she at Merhavia that within a year of her arrival she was elected to the steering committee that supervised kibbutz life. Chosen to represent Merhavia at a kibbutz convention in 1922, she met kibbutzniks from all over Palestine. Golda also served as Merhavia's delegate to the Histadrut, the Jewish trade union in Palestine. Soon Golda was again traveling and speaking at conferences and committee meetings. Her gift for clear, persuasive speech, her enthusiasm, and her dedication attracted the attention of many of the Jewish community's labor leaders, men who were to become the nucleus of the Jewish government in Palestine.

But as Golda's spirits soared, her husband's plummeted. He had contracted malaria early in their stay and still spent several days a month shivering with fever. Heavy labor had given him a hernia, and his stomach rebelled against the coarse food and Spartan regimen. Morris also felt the intellectual limitations of kibbutz life. No one else in the group talked about music or literature; they came to life only if the topic was farm equipment or politics. He felt that his comrades were too narrow in their outlook, too earnest, as if somehow they'd developed the idea that a sense of humor was inappropriate to their goals.

Most of all, he suffered from a lack of privacy. He rarely saw Golda alone and sorely missed having time to sit with her and share a pot of tea in the quiet of their own room. He took to writing long and bitter letters to his mother in America. Who else would listen to Morris's complaints? His wife was too involved in the community to pay attention to his unhappiness. It was not until many years later that Golda realized she had deprived him of the love and support he needed to adapt to a way of life that was physically and emotionally hard for him. At the time, however, she saw only her own needs clearly.

A letter from her father suddenly woke her from her dream. Golda had written excitedly about one of the kibbutz cows that had just produced a lovely little calf. "Wonderful," replied her father. "And when are *you* going to imitate the cow?"

Moshe had poked at a very sensitive spot with his little joke. Golda and Morris wanted to have a baby very badly. Morris, however, would not even consider raising a family on a kibbutz. He wanted to bring up his children as he saw fit, and not according to the collective decisions of the kibbutzniks. He wanted to hold his children, feed them, play with them, teach them, and watch them grow, but kibbutz children are reared in children's houses and cared for by all the parents in turn. If Golda really wanted a baby, they'd have to leave Merhavia.

The Myersons had been married six years by now. During all that time Golda had been free to pursue her desires, and Morris had gone along with her each time. Now there was something he wanted to pursue—a family and a "normal" home. Could she, in fairness, say no? Besides, she told herself, he really wasn't well enough to work at Merhavia any longer. Perhaps leaving would renew both his health and their marriage. So with a heavy heart she packed up their belongings for the third time in three years.

They moved back to Tel Aviv and looked for work. It was not a happy time. Both of them felt restless and depressed. Morris blamed Golda for ruining his health, and she resented his making her leave the kibbutz where she was happy and useful. Then, on the very day Golda learned she was pregnant, a friend offered them both jobs with Solel Boneh, a construction company that trained and employed Jewish workers in the building trades. Golda could be a cashier in the office until the baby was born, and Morris could be a bookkeeper. While the jobs meant they would have to move to Jerusalem, neither complained. Golda believed they would be happier in the next place.

The Myersons found a two-room apartment in the ultra-religious Jewish neighborhood on the outskirts of Jerusalem.

Their new quarters had neither gas nor electricity; each night Golda lit oil lamps and cooked over a tiny oil camp stove. All the tenants of the building shared a bathroom and a large tin-walled kitchen in the back yard.

Golda, Morris, and their son Menachem, born in November 1924, lived in one room. A boarder had the other. There was no other way to meet the rent, for Morris's pay envelope usually held IOUs instead of the cash that the landlord preferred. Most shopkeepers favored hard currency, too. While Golda learned to juggle the piasters and pounds of Palestinian money to keep food on the table, at the end of the month they always faced a disturbing pile of petty bills.

Golda had been poor and hungry before. But this daily struggle for necessities was new to her, and, unlike the austerity she had so gladly embraced at Merhavia, it was totally without redeeming benefit or glamour. Golda also missed the support and companionship of her comrades. Worn out by worry and the demands of her baby, Golda took Menachem back to Merhavia in the spring of 1925, thinking she'd feel more like her old self there. But even in the busy, happy hubbub, Golda was torn between her duty to her husband, child, and home and her desire to live the kind of life she really wanted and needed. "Not for the first time," she wrote, "and certainly not for the last, I realized that in a conflict between my duty and my innermost desires, it was my duty that had the prior claim."

She returned to Morris and Jerusalem after six months, determined to try again to be the kind of wife he needed. When their daughter Sarah was born in May 1926, life became even harder for Golda. There was no longer enough space in the apartment for all of them, and so the boarder left, taking with him that essential cash.

Now Golda worried all the time about making do with Morris's wages. Cramped in their tiny rooms, she feared not having the money to feed and house her children decently. She was getting good at persuading the grocer to wait a little longer for his money, and at buying milk and bread on credit. Whenever she had a few extra piasters, she'd buy bones from the butcher and make soup, saving the little scraps of meat for Sarah and Menachem.

Despite her anxieties, Golda met her difficulties with competence and vigor. The apartment might be small, but it was clean; the clothes might be threadbare, but they were neatly pressed; the meal might be meager, but it was tasty. She also looked for other ways of obtaining what she wanted. In exchange for Menachem's tuition at nursery school, Golda did the school's laundry. Later, in order to teach English at a private school, Golda took her children to work with her, for baby-sitters were not in the Myerson budget.

Golda began to see herself as a prisoner sentenced to a lifetime of poverty, drudgery, and worry. To please Morris she had withdrawn from the world and devoted herself to her family, but four years of this life had not changed her as Morris had hoped. Every day her dissatisfaction grew. It wasn't that she didn't believe that being a good mother was the most important job in the world. It just wasn't enough of a job for her. Nor was marriage. Golda's tremendous need to do, to give, and to build welled up in her, and she started to resent her "life of so little meaning." She'd come to Palestine to build the Jewish homeland, not to change diapers and wipe noses. Overwhelmed by her frustration and isolation, Golda saw that for her own sanity she'd have to work, not at the menial jobs with which she'd been supplementing Morris's income, but at meaningful, challenging tasks.

But work was not going to be easy to find. Hard times had hit Jewish Palestine. By 1927, seven thousand men and women, five percent of the *yishuv,* were out of work, and more people left Palestine than came to it. There simply wasn't enough Jewish capital and industry to employ the Jewish labor force, and those jobs that were open were likely to be filled by Arabs, who were willing to work for much lower wages. All over the country construction came to a halt. Lines of unemployed workers looking for jobs wound around half-built apartment houses and down partially paved roads.

The British mandatory government, bowing to pressure from Arab nationalists, refused to help. It was up to the Jews themselves to build their own country. But with little or no experience in self-government or industry, and funded only by Zionist groups abroad, the leaders of the Histadrut and other Jewish organizations were lost. It seemed to Golda that the golden dreams of the earlier settlers were dying, and she yearned to revive them.

Cautiously she told a few friends she was thinking of going back to work. Within days the same man who had arranged the Solel Boneh jobs heard of her interest and called her into his office. Expressing his delight at her decision, he added that the Zionist movement couldn't afford to let Golda's talents go unused. Then he asked her to become secretary of Moetzet Hapoalot, the Women's Labor Council of the Histadrut, or Jewish Labor Federation in Palestine.

By now the Histadrut was more than a labor union. Representing half of the Jewish workers in Palestine, its aims went beyond the concerns of trade unions and into the creation of a viable national economy based on the unity of *all* workers in the *yishuv,* from farmhands to kibbutzniks to professors. By themselves the members of the Histadrut accepted the responsibility of solving the problems of industry, finance, transportation, construction, welfare, unemployment, and immigration. With income from members' dues, it built factories, paved roads, organized and ran several schools, operated a publishing house, and printed a newspaper. Because it touched so many areas of Palestinian life, the Histadrut acted as the *yishuv* government and helped Palestinian Jews fulfill their part of the Balfour Declaration by establishing their own agencies and providing the means to support them. In accepting this job, Golda knew she would be in the forefront of these efforts to build a strong Jewish state.

How could she say no to such a chance? She took the post on the spot and excitedly made her way home through the crowded streets to tell her family. The children didn't understand much of her talk about their moving back to Tel Aviv, and her traveling all over the country and maybe abroad, but Morris did. And even though Golda optimistically announced that once she was happier she would be a better wife and mother, Morris knew that this was the beginning of the end for them.

He understood better than she did that Golda could never be the wife he wanted. Their marriage had been doomed from the start. Two such opposite personalities could never live in real harmony. Their tragedy was that neither of them ever had the strength to make a clean break. Golda's job helped them separate, and, although they never divorced, the Myersons never lived together again. Morris remained a loving, supportive husband and father, but Golda never overcame her guilt at not being able to make their marriage work. This guilt was compounded in 1951 when Morris died at Golda's house while visiting the children. Golda, characteristically, was away. At his funeral she remembered a wry joke Morris had once made: "I came to Palestine to be with Golda, but she was never there."

Golda threw herself into her job with all the energy and enthusiasm she'd pent up during her four unhappy years in Jerusalem. Her work was interesting and made good use of her talent for organization. She developed "working women's farms" where immigrant girls could be trained for agricultural work and could learn Hebrew, at a time when few women were trained for anything at all. She instituted day-care centers and kindergartens where women could leave their children while they worked. Golda journeyed throughout Palestine visiting these programs, and she toured Europe and America bringing the Zionist message to women who would never see the projects she was asking them to sponsor.

Golda was the ideal person for this position. Young and attractive, her American background coupled with almost ten years' hard experience in Palestine made her a dynamic speaker. Her eloquence in Yiddish, Hebrew, and English only broadened her appeal and made her an invaluable ambassador to England and the United States. The Moetzet Hapoalot recognized its find and sent her to more and more meetings, conferences, and fund-raising events.

Her work brought her great satisfaction, but even greater heartaches. It left her with little time or energy for her children, and now there was no one else to help take care of them. Golda tried to be everything to Sarah and Menachem during those precious hours when her work was done. She took them to music lessons and doctor's appointments, read to them, played with them, but always wondered if she wasn't harming them nevertheless.

For although her children accepted their mother's frequent absences intellectually, they still resented her job and particularly dreaded her long journeys abroad. On the rare days when Golda stayed home from the office (which she never did unless she was ill), Sarah and Menachem would serenade her with a joyous song they had composed for such occasions. Its words were simple: "Mommy's staying home today! Mommy has a headache! Mommy's staying home today!" It was certainly not a song to make the head—or the heart—of the woman lying on the couch feel any better.

Yet Golda learned to live with her feelings of guilt about her children. Writing anonymously in a journal called *The Ploughwoman* in 1930, Golda described the anguish and struggles of working mothers. She pictured both those women who are forced to work because of economic necessity, and those like herself:

> There is a type of woman who cannot remain home for other reasons. In spite of the place which her children and her family take up in her life, her nature and being demand something more; . . . She cannot let her children narrow her horizon. And for such a woman there is no rest. . . . The mother suffers in the very work she has taken up. Always she has the feeling that her work is not as good or productive as that of a man or even of an unmarried woman. The children, too, demand her in health, and even more in sickness. And this inner division, this double pull, this alternating feeling of unfulfilled duty—today toward her family, the next day toward her work—this is the burden of the working mother.

Unfortunately, Golda got little emotional support for this life she had chosen. Both her sister Sheyna and her parents (who had come to Palestine to live in 1926) were willing to help with the baby-sitting, but Golda paid for this service by enduring long lectures about how she was depriving her children of a real mother. Sheyna was particularly disapproving of her younger sister's activities, and in one stern letter accused her of turning into a "public person, not a homebody," as any good mother should be. Now, besides overcoming her own turmoil, Golda had to defend herself to the one person whose good opinion meant the most to her.

In a reply written while at a foreign conference, Golda assured Sheyna that she never would have gone if the children were not adequately cared for; her maternal responsibilities still came first. But, she explained, her work was an "absolute necessity" for her, and for Palestine: "In our present situation I could not refuse to do what was asked of me . . . we must miss no opportunity to explain to influential people what we want and what we are."

"I could not refuse to do what was asked of me." These words became Golda's credo, her rationale for devoting her life to her country, no matter what. Even when Sarah became critically ill, Golda did not withdraw from her public duties. In fact, she took on more.

Early in 1932, Sarah began running a constant fever. The doctors in Tel Aviv diagnosed a specific kidney ailment and put the child on a liquid diet. Poor Sarah would sit in bed and pretend that one glass of water was a bowl of oatmeal and another a crispy golden chicken wing. Golda and Morris each saw that the therapy wasn't working; their daughter was fading before their eyes. Sarah needed expert medical care, the kind available only in the United States. As neither parent could afford the trip, Golda went to the leadership of the Moetzet Hapoalot and asked to be sent as an emissary to their sister organization in America, the Pioneer Women. She would take the children with her, and Sarah could go to one of the best hospitals in the world.

Her superiors were delighted with Golda's offer. They needed someone to broaden the membership of Pioneer Women, to fill them with enough enthusiasm for the goals of Zionism and Palestine to make them an even more effective fund-raising arm of the Moetzet Hapoalot. They agreed to send her to New York for two years.

Spurred by Sarah's worsening condition, Golda quickly got her tickets and arrangements in order. Both family and doctors told her she was mad to take such a sick child halfway around the world, but Golda was desperate. Her children endured the long trip with good grace, sensing the terrible strain and worry their mother bore, and knowing that every night she dragged a deck chair down to their cabin and sat up until the dawn, watching over their little forms in the bunks.

Once in New York, Golda left Menachem with friends in Brooklyn and took Sarah to Beth Israel Hospital in Manhattan. Neither child spoke any English, yet both suddenly found themselves alone in an English-speaking world. Menachem, at least, could make himself understood in his immediate neighborhood in Yiddish, for he was surrounded by Jews. But Sarah had no one. Mothers were not permitted to stay with their children, and Sarah screamed at the end of each of Golda's visits. The tiny six-year-old had to overcome the terror not only of being among strangers but of being alone in the hospital as well.

Fortunately her stay was short. The American doctors quickly realized that Sarah's disease was less severe than the Palestinians had thought, and they changed her treatment to include a well-balanced diet and plenty of exercise. Within weeks Sarah was a plump, red-cheeked little girl, reunited with her brother in Brooklyn, and her grateful mother was ready to begin work in earnest.

During the two years she spent in the United States as national secretary of the Pioneer Women, Golda crisscrossed the continent many times. She made speeches at tea parties, ate chicken at charity banquets, and packaged Passover matzo for fund raisers. Sometimes she had three engagements in two days, with only time for a catnap at a hostess's house between. At every stop new recruits joined up, new chapters organized themselves, and benefits and projects got under way. Golda's straightforward, unsentimental approach worked impressively, and the Pioneer Women raised

*Golda (second row, second from left)
with leaders of the Pioneer Women, the
American organization in which Golda served
as national secretary from 1932 to 1934*

more money for their Palestinian sisters than anyone had imagined possible.

But by 1934 Golda was tired of her schedule and her job. It was time to go home. Gathering her Americanized, bilingual children, she packed their toys, clothes, and Menachem's new cello and sailed back to Palestine, eager to move on to a new challenge.

NO PLACE
TO GO

4

Working for Moetzet Hapoalot was the first and last job Golda ever had with a women's organization. From there she went on to other national activities, always on an equal footing with her male colleagues. She neither asked special favors nor claimed unfair disadvantages because of her sex. "Being a woman never hindered me in any way at all," she said, but added that she often had a "much, much harder time than men" because of her "heavy double burden."

Regardless of the weight of this burden, Golda did not hesitate at all when, within weeks of her return to Palestine, she was offered a place on Vaad Hapoel, the executive committee of the Histadrut and, as such, the unofficial cabinet of the *yishuv* government. Her first assignment was to direct the Department of Tourism. No, Palestine was not a fashionable resort in the 1930s. Planeloads, or boat- or trainloads, of vacationers did not descend on Jerusalem and Tel Aviv. But foreign government officials, military men, Zionist and socialist leaders did come to Palestine, eager to see what the Jews had accomplished in this desolate and neglected corner of the Middle East. Golda arranged their transportation and lodging, introduced them to the people they wanted to meet, showed them around a kibbutz, and guided them through a school or factory. Although this was a job she enjoyed, Golda kept it for less then a year.

She moved closer to the inner circle of Palestinian leadership in 1935, when she became a member of Vaad Hapoel's secretariat, or steering committee. From this position Golda managed all the Histadrut's mutual-aid programs and served as chairman of the board for Kupat Holim, the Worker's Sick Fund that protected forty percent of the population. She also directed the pension fund investments and eventually became head of the Trade Union and Labor Relations Council.

Each new job came with more responsibility and more pressure, but Golda's eye for detail and genius for organization helped her meet their challenges. Fortunately, too, she never seemed to run out of emotional or physical energy for the long hours she kept; in fact, she thrived on her diet of meetings and hard work.

Golda's rise as a Histadrut leader was not always an easy climb. Her directness and stubbornness irritated some colleagues. And she never courted the public by approving programs she didn't agree with, even at the risk of losing her popularity and position.

Nor was she afraid to champion causes that were bound to make the yishuv grumble. One of these was the family wage scale. In those days every worker started with the same fixed wage, and it increased only with his or her seniority and number of dependents. In other words, workers were paid according to their needs. By the 1930s, however, lawyers and nurses began to feel they deserved more than truckers and janitors,and they pressured the Histadrut to change the rates. Golda, the dedicated socialist, held out for the fixed wage, unworkable as it may have been, for she held that it was essential for true equality. To her, increments belonged only to those with more mouths to feed or feet to shoe.

Another unpopular cause she crusaded for was an unemployment fund. The Zionist dream of living in dignity in

Palestine could not be realized while so many were out of work. It was, she felt, the duty of those with jobs to help those without. Golda lobbied hard in Vaad Hapoel for permission to set up a program she called Mifdeh, the Hebrew word for redemption. Employed members of the Histadrut gave up one day's wages a month to the fund—with a great deal of complaining. This was their union levying the tax, after all, not their country. Golda countered their objections by reminding everyone that hardship was part of their pioneer tradition, and, in spite of the opposition, the fund prospered. Later in the 1930s, when ten thousand workers stood idle, the Histadrut started Mifdeh B, an increase in the tax, with scarcely a whimper from its membership. The Mifdeh also served as a precedent for Hofer Hayishuv (ransom of the *yishuv*), a defense tax imposed on the entire *yishuv*, and for various war needs and rescue funds. By applying socialist principles to Palestinian problems, Golda was helping the *yishuv* act like the country it aspired to be.

After a full day of administering the sick fund, checking on factory conditions, or negotiating contracts, Golda took the bus home to her other job. She gave her evening and early morning hours to cooking and shopping, to housework and homework; in short, to motherhood.

The three Myersons rented a two-room apartment in a new cement-block building on a recently paved street in Tel Aviv. The children shared one room, and Golda slept on a couch in the other. A small terrace helped the place seem larger and airier.

Sarah and Menachem now went to a Histadrut school whose hours coincided with an adult's working day, so Golda didn't have to worry so much about baby-sitters. When she traveled she still relied on her mother or sister to watch them, however.

Morris was living and working in Haifa, where he had spent his family's American sojourn. Devoted to his children, and especially delighted by Menachem's musical gifts, he journeyed to Tel Aviv each weekend to share the Sabbath with them. On Friday afternnons Sarah and Menachem would race home from school to wait for him at the bus stop. After the hugging and kissing, the three of them would stroll, chatting and laughing, to their favorite bookstore. There Morris bought each child a book, collected his foreign newspapers and magazines, and browsed happily among the crowded shelves, choosing his reading for the coming week. By sundown they were at the apartment for the festive Sabbath dinner that Golda, like Jewish housewives all over the world, had cooked. On Saturday they relaxed and visited with friends and relatives, and late that night Morris would board the Haifa bus again, waving sadly to the family he would miss for another week.

Such an arrangement—a part-time father and an overworked mother—was hard on the children. Yet Sarah and Menachem learned to accept their unhappiness, and also how to be on their own. Their mother's career also showed them the importance and satisfaction of being associated with worthwhile causes. But neither child, however proud of Golda's prominence in *yishuv* affairs, ever felt happy enough to boast about her position. In fact, whenever they were asked about their mother's occupation, they just mumbled that their mother worked for the Histadrut.

In 1937 the Histadrut undertook a new project called Nachshon. Nachshon, legend had it, was the first Jew to follow Moses into the Red Sea during the Exodus from Egypt. Now the Jews, landlocked in ghettos for centuries, were going to enter the sea again by developing their own shipping and fishing industries. But the Histradrut needed money to train Jewish sailors, buy Jewish ships, and open Jewish ports. Golda, who had ably proved herself as a fund raiser with the Pioneer Women, was sent back to the United States to raise the money. For months before she left, she gathered the information she'd present to her American audience. Tonnage charts and coastal maps slipcovered her couch; deck plans draped her tables; and engineering books made tidy towers on the floor. Her enthusiasm and expertise swayed the American Jews to open their wallets again, and she returned to Palestine with enough money to start building a seaport at Tel Aviv.

During the months of construction, ships and the sea were the main topic of conversation in Tel Aviv and its nearby villages. On pleasant evenings and sunny Sabbaths, citizens pursued their favorite pastime, strolling down to the Mediterranean and checking what progress had been made. The day the first ship tied up at the long wooden jetty was one of great excitement. Half the city turned out to cheer the Jewish longshoremen as they unloaded dusty sacks of concrete from an old Yugoslav freighter. The port of Tel Aviv became a source of pride and a symbol of independence for the *yishuv*. More than a demonstration of what they could accomplish, it represented another foundation stone in their economy, a chance to provide jobs and compete in the world markets.

Golda went back to America shortly after the port opened. This time she wanted to raise money to buy ships—for fishing and trade, she said. But she, and the rest of the *yishuv*, had a more urgent use for boats of any size. They needed them to rescue European Jews and bring them safely to Palestine.

For in 1933, Adolf Hitler became head of the German government. Hitler believed in the supremacy of the German people, and he vowed to restore his nation to the wealth and power it had enjoyed before the First World War. In order to do this, he insisted, he first had to purify the race, to weed out of German society anyone who was not of solid Aryan stock. Hitler and his Nazi party passed laws persecuting the members of many ethnic and religious groups, but none so severely as the Jews.

Hitler made anti-Semitism fashionable. Signs began to appear on park benches and in shop windows: "We do not serve Jews," "No Jews allowed," "Jews—and dogs—not welcome here." Huge bonfires consumed books by Jewish authors; orchestras discarded scores by Jewish composers. Jewish children were transferred to special schools, while their parents lost their jobs, their businesses, and their property. Jews could no longer buy food or medicine easily, or even talk freely in the streets. Synagogues and temples were burned and looted. With the passage of the Nuremberg Laws in 1935, the German Jews lost the rest of their civil rights. To make them more visible, they now had to wear yellow Stars of David on their coats and live in ghettos. The number of people affected by this persecution was far greater than the actual number of practicing Jews in Germany. To make sure he was eradicating every trace of Jewishness, Hitler defined a Jew as anyone, religious or not, having at least one Jewish grandparent.

Hitler originally planned to evacuate Jews from German lands, and his policies succeeded in driving many away on their own. Some escaped to neighboring countries, some to America. And sixty thousand came to Palestine, arriving thankfully on its shores with nothing but their lives and the clothes on their backs.

Since 1934, when the Youth Aliyah began rescuing European Jewish children from the Nazis and placing them in children's villages and foster homes in Palestine, the *yishuv* had been accommodating thousands of young people whose parents, desperate to save them at all costs, had made the heartbreaking decision to send them away. But children are one thing; adults, another. How could a population of four hundred thousand hope to absorb a group one-sixth its size? How quickly could they take these German lawyers, musicians, and merchants and turn them into the Hebrew-speaking farmers, truckers, and bricklayers the *yishuv* so badly needed? It was not easy for anyone, but Golda and her colleagues had to make a place for them; there was no place else in the world for them to go. Working beyond the point of exhaustion, they housed, fed, and found jobs for the refugees all over the country.

The newcomers soon realized that they had fled from one nightmare to another. Their new home was constantly under siege by its Arab neighbors. Kibbutzniks dug trenches and strung barbed wire around their frail settlements. Armed guards patrolled the fields, and no one wore white at night. It made too easy a target for a sniper's bullet. Arab guerrillas overturned Jewish buses, looted Jewish shops, and destroyed hundreds of thousands of tiny trees planted by hopeful pioneers. Jews began to keep piles of stones in their houses for defense in case of riots or fights. Things were so bad that when Golda kissed the children good-bye in the morning and drove to Jerusalem for a meeting, she wasn't sure she'd be alive to kiss them good night.

Arab hostility had always been a fact of life for the *yishuv*. The clash of European and Middle Eastern cultures made some conflict inevitable, but in the beginning some Jews and Arabs had seen Zionism as good, pan-Semitic cooperation. In fact, shortly after World War I, the Saudi Arabian King Faisal publicly welcomed the Jews home.

But other Arab nationalist leaders feared that Jewish expansion would cost them their lands. They felt threatened and angry; the violence and riots that had erupted sporadically through the years raged more frequently now. During the early thirties, Arabs made more than two thousand attacks on Jews and burned countless fields and homes.

In all of this the Jews maintained a strict policy of nonretaliation. The Haganah, the *yishuv*'s defense force, protected farm settlements with manpower and guns, but never answered violence with more violence. This policy of turning the other cheek was grounded in the Jewish belief that terror is morally abhorrent. Self-restraint was a practical response, too. The Jews feared that if they played too active a role in their own defense, the British would punish them by clamping down on Jewish immigration and settlement. Some Jews disagreed, but most realized that it was up to them to act with pride, dignity, and reason in the face of these attacks.

This unofficial and undeclared war reached a peak in 1936 when, after weeks of disturbances, the Arab Higher Committee announced a general strike, forbidding any Arab in Palestine to work until Jewish immigration and land purchases stopped altogether. By paralyzing the *yishuv* and its economy, the Arabs figured on a rapid surrender to their demands.

But the Jews had too much at stake to give in. Their response to the strike was to take over the Arabs' jobs themselves, and they willingly climbed behind the wheels of idle trucks and buses. Farmers planted double and triple crops to make up for fallow Arab fields. Men and women waited on tables, delivered groceries, and answered telephones. And the new port of Tel Aviv handled the traffic from the Arab-run port of Jaffa.

The British, who had been the government in Palestine since 1917–18, tried to control the chaos by limiting Jewish immigration. Unwilling to forfeit their own powerful influence in the Middle East, they finally gave in to the Arabs as completely as they had given in to Hitler at Munich in 1938, and, in May 1939, issued the White Paper. This document signaled the end of the British mandate in the troubled country by calling for the creation of an independent Palestinian nation within the next ten years. This new country would have a constitution guaranteeing the rights of its Christian and Jewish minorities. The White Paper also restricted Jewish land purchases to all but five percent of Palestine. But the most devastating proviso was the one that ended immigration. To make sure that there would always be an Arab majority, only seventy-five thousand Jews could enter Palestine in each of the next five years. After that, immigration was to stop forever, "unless the Arabs of Palestine are prepared to acquiesce in it."

The White Paper was published just after Golda returned from an international conference on refugees in France, which had met to find ways of rescuing the victims of Hitler's persecution. In horror she had watched as one by one the representatives of thirty-two nations walked up to the podium and, in kind words, expressed their sympathy with the plight of the Jews and their regrets that they could not offer them asylum.

Golda was frantic. Where could these poor people go? As the Jewish observer from Palestine, not its delegate, she had no official voice at the conference. She tried behind-the-scenes lobbying, but not one delegate changed his mind. In fact, several admitted that their governments had forbidden them to. The call to action had devolved into an enormous apology. Bitterly angry and frustrated, Golda called a press conference before going home. If she couldn't register her outrage at the sessions, she'd broadcast it to the world.

"There is only one thing I hope to see before I die," she summed up for the reporters and photograhers clustered around her, "and that is that my people should not need expressions of sympathy any more."

At that time there were only two nations willing to take the refugees: Palestine and the United States. But the United States wouldn't raise its immigration quota to accommodate the thousands facing internment in concentration camps. And Palestine, the one place eager to receive the Jews, willing and ready to do whatever was necessary to rescue them, was virtually closed to them by the White Paper. Places for seventy-five thousand were hardly enough when millions were threatened.

By the late summer of 1939, when Golda went to Geneva, Switzerland, for what was to be the last Zionist Congress before World War II, she was able to report to her comrades that, rather than join the list of nations that "bitterly regretted" their inability to help the Jews, the *yishuv* had decided to continue immigration, settlement, and self-defense—no matter what Arab reprisals this might elicit, no matter that such a policy was bound to lead to armed clashes with the British. David Ben-Gurion, head of the large and popular Mapai party, put the matter simply: "Jews should act as though we were the state in Palestine, and should so act until there will be a Jewish state." The Refugee Conference and the White Paper had taught the Jews two very important lessons. One was that no foreign government would ever value Jewish lives as Jews themselves did. The other was that independence was no longer a luxury. No longer could uncomprehending strangers make the rules for them. Lives depended on Jewish control of their country and its immigration laws.

Few of the Zionists at the congress lived to see a Jewish nation. Leaving Switzerland for their homes in France, Poland, and Holland, they were to fight the Nazi invaders in the ghettos and in the streets until they, too, became part of Hitler's "final solution." Rounded up and herded into boxcars with millions of other Jews, they were to find themselves behind the electrified barbed-wire fences of Dachau, Auschwitz, and

Buchenwald, where the Nazis systematically burned or gassed the inmates or even buried them alive to make the world truly *judenrein*—free of Jews.

Once war broke out in September 1939, it became almost impossible for the *yishuv* to keep in touch with family, friends, and colleagues in Europe. A terrible, impenetrable silence shrouded the continent, broken only by battle reports and scattered stories about the camps, stories so horrible that few people believed them. Could the Nazis really have pulled seventeen tons of gold out of the teeth of Jewish corpses at Auschwitz? Could they really be using human hair to stuff mattresses, human fat to make soap, human ashes for fertilizer? People didn't do such things. Monstrous evil of that sort couldn't exist.

Golda remembered "distinctly the day that those first awful reports reached us about the gas chambers and the soap and the lampshades that were being made from Jewish bodies. We held an emergency meeting. . . . The curious and terrible thing was that none of us questioned the information we had received. We all believed the reports immediately and in their entirety." But she refused to surrender to despair or sorrow, and set to work trying to reestablish contact with European Jews through any means. As Golda declared: "There is no Zionism save the rescue of the Jews."

That would be difficult enough. All efforts to get the White Paper suspended failed. The British first politely ignored, then forcefully denied Jewish requests to take in as many Jews as still could be saved from the Nazis. Good relations with the Arabs were still paramount, despite the chief Arab leader's close ties with the very man the British were committed to defeating, Adolf Hitler. The *yishuv* had no choice then but to resist. David Ben-Gurion again gave them a rallying cry: "We shall fight the war as if there were no White Paper, and fight the White Paper as if there were no war."

That brave statement sums up all the contradictions and confusions in Palestine from 1939 to 1945. The *yishuv* found itself at once fighting against and with the British. While opposing British policy and smuggling Jews into Palestine, they also tried to convince the Crown to let them fight Hitler under the Union Jack. And at the same time, the *yishuv* had to keep up its economy, to handle the postwar refugees.

As a member of Vaad Hapoel, Golda worked hard on all three fronts. Her children saw her less than ever, as meetings filled her long days and longer nights. She sat on the War Economic Advisory Council, which the British had set up. She helped raise 75,000 pounds for the Vaad Hapoel to pass to European Jews for food and arms. And while she was resting, she wrote anti-British pamphlets and flyers for the Haganah, which her children secretly distributed by day.

The Haganah had grown tremendously during the war. No longer merely the *yishuv*'s band of watchmen, it was now widely based among the Jewish population and functioned under Histadrut rule. Yet, although almost everyone belonged to it and worked for it in some capacity, the Haganah was still a clandestine operation. It had to be, for it had declared the gathering of refugees to be equally as important to the *yishuv* as the settlement of the land and self-defense, thereby actively opposing the White Paper and the mandatory government.

The Haganah used about sixty ships to bring immigrants to Palestine. Many nights, civilians lined the beaches, straining their eyes for a distant vessel, wading into the water to aid the frightened passengers who had to be landed silently and secretly. Others waited with trucks and cars to take the new arrivals to farms and villages inland. Golda herself spent many hours on the terrace of her apartment, her binoculars fixed on the white caps on the dark sea, watching the rescue. The British, determined to enforce the White Paper, hunted Haganah members as ruthlessly as they searched for illegal immigrants, sending the refugees back to Europe and the Haganah to jail. But the threat of imprisonment stopped no one.

The Haganah made a last bold effort to reach their brothers and sisters in Europe in 1943. Volunteers parachuted behind enemy lines, planning to aid Jews, partisans, and prisoners of war and to bring hope to those in the camps. Most of the thirty-two men and women, among them several of Golda's friends and rising leaders of the *yishuv*, were captured and killed almost immediately upon landing.

Although the Jews had accepted the war as theirs to fight, the British army refused to let them volunteer. But as the German forces drew nearer to the Middle East and seemed ready to invade Egypt and Palestine, they changed their minds. First the British recruited Jews to drive buses, fix equipment, and help doctors. Then, once the advantages of a trained and trustworthy native unit became apparent, they organized the Palmach, commando units that were to help the army in case of invasion. It wasn't until 1944, after the Allies landed in Italy, that the Jews were finally allowed to serve in the army, and the Jewish Brigade with its Star of David shoulder patch soon became a brave symbol throughout Europe.

Anguish and anxiety marked the war years for Golda. Driven by fear and desperation, she worked harder than ever before. Each day she learned that she could go beyond what she thought was yesterday's limit of endurance. Never doubting either the Allied victory or the survival of the Jewish people, she and the other Palestinian leaders coped with their sorrow by planning for the years ahead, when they would have their own nation and there would never again be any such thing as a Jewish refugee.

ERETZ
ISRAEL

5

When, on May 8, 1945, Germany surrendered to the Allies and peace was declared in Europe, the world rejoiced. In New York, London, Paris, and Moscow, people spilled out of buildings and onto the pavement, weeping with joy, hugging strangers, singing and dancing. Bells and sirens rang joyously through the air, thankful prayers filled churches, and flags fluttered bravely from almost every window.

They celebrated in Palestine, too. Crowds of young people thronged the streets, dancing the hora and singing patriotic songs well into the night. But many Jews could not join them. However thankful they might have been that the fighting and killing had stopped, they had lost too much to be able to share the festivities. How could they dance, when one-third of their people had been trapped and destroyed by Hitler's murderous machines? And the *yishuv* mourned not only the loss of these six million men, women, and children, but also the generations that now would never be born.

The doomed victims of the Holocaust had shown the *yishuv* the absolute necessity of being in charge of their own affairs. Out of their ashes rose the phoenix of the *yishuv*'s resolve to have their own nation. As Golda recalled, their only consolation was the hope of creating a land with "such moral values, such decency and human dignity that all the people who had hated and persecuted us down the centuries will come to us to learn the meaning of human dignity and human decency."

The *yishuv* believed, perhaps naively, that their goal was about to be achieved. Surely the horrified but enlightened postwar world would now understand their need for nation-hood and act to prevent the recurrence of such human devastation. The Palestinian Jews were even more encour-aged when, in 1946, President Harry Truman declared that the United States supported the creation of a Jewish state.

But Truman stood alone. The British, still in control of Palestine, refused to rescind the White Paper. They had care-fully issued the designated number of immigration permits each month all during the war and intended to keep doing so until they'd all been used; then Palestine would be closed to any more Jews. Deaf to the *yishuv*'s pleas that they immedi-ately allow in one hundred thousand displaced persons (the postwar euphemism for refugees), the British patrolled the coastline even more thoroughly, sending any illegal arrivals to internment camps on Cyprus or, when these were filled, back to hastily converted and renamed concentration camps in Germany.

The *yishuv* kept smuggling boatloads of refugees into Palestine. Following Ben-Gurion's advice, they had fought the war and won. Now it was time to defeat the White Paper.

Recognizing the extent of the *yishuv*'s antagonism, the British called an Anglo-American committee to resolve the refugee problem and agreed to abide by its recommenda-tions. Twelve prominent men from the United States and Great Britain were duly selected and sent to Palestine to study the question. They stopped first, however, at some of the D.P. (displaced persons) camps in Europe. Horrified by the primitive conditions they found, the commissioners were even more appalled when they talked with the inmates. These

Jews, strained to the breaking point, spoke only of going to Palestine. Their children sat in makeshift schools, keeping away despair by studying maps of the countryside and singing heartbreaking songs about "Our Land." For Europe, the cemetery of their people, was no longer home. Very few cared even to go to the United States. Almost everyone the commissioners interviewed listed only two places on earth they wanted: Palestine or the grave.

Sobered by their findings, the commissioners visited the Arab states to hear their side. The Middle East at this time was home to fifty million Arabs, yet they feared one state of a million Jews. The newly United Arab League sent a statement ot its opposition to Jewish immigration, but the member states did nothing more to cooperate.

The committee finally opened hearings at the Jerusalem YMCA in March 1946. They called both Arab and Jewish Palestinians to answer questions and explain their positions. The representative of the Histadrut, and the only woman to testify, was Golda Myerson.

She, along with the other *yishuv* leaders, was skeptical about the sensitivity these gentlemen would bring to their deliberations. In her opening remarks she asked if, for all their good intentions, they could "realize what it means to be a member of a people whose very right to exist is constantly being threatened." Speaking of all the Jews who would have lived if they had been allowed to come to Palestine, and of the *yishuv*'s bitterness at being able to save only the relatively few illegal immigrants, Golda went on to champion the right of the remaining Jewish children to come to Palestine and grow up without fear. "We Jews," she said, "only want that which is given naturally to all the peoples of the world, to be masters of our own fate."

Clearly and directly she affirmed that all six hundred thousand Jews in Palestine would do whatever they had to in order to absorb the battered remnant of European Jewry. Politely but firmly she answered all questions, even when she was bristling underneath. When one commissioner asked her why they had chosen Hebrew as a national language, she pointed out to him that it was the Jews' common tongue, just as English was the Englishmen's and French the Frenchmen's. But she flatly rejected the suggestion that the Jews might be content with a protected minority status in an Arab Palestinian state. "There must be one place where Jews are *not* a minority," she insisted. They'd been plagued by the curse of being a minority all over the world, and all it had brought them was persecution, helplessness, and lack of dignity. Somewhere it had to be different.

As the commissioners deliberated, the *yishuv* grew more dispirited daily. The world, following the Nuremberg trials of Nazi war criminals, took the stories of Hitler's atrocities with astonishing calm. The refugees still huddled in their barracks, cold, hungry, and without hope. And weren't half of the commissioners British? What good could possibly come of this genteel inquiry?

A new crisis soon took everyone's attention from the committee. The British, determined to stop illegal immigration at its source, started turning the refugees back to the D.P. camps before the ships ever left their European ports. In April 1946 they caught an old Haganah vessel, the *Fede,* crammed with twelve hundred refugees, and pressured the Italian authorities to hold it in the port of La Spezia. But the *Fede*'s passengers refused to cooperate. They would not disembark; they threatened to blow up the ship; and finally they stopped eating.

Golda, representing the Vaad Hapoel to the Vaad Leumi (the National Council), urged those leaders to join the *Fede* hunger strike, both to prove their solidarity with their homeless brethren and to focus world attention on the tragedy of the situation. The council agreed unanimously to allow fifteen strikers, one from each major organization in the *yishuv*, to join—but only with medical clearance.

The strike nearly foundered here. Not many doctors, no matter how strong their Zionist sympathies, can comfortably tell a patient it's all right to starve himself or herself. One man, faced with an uncooperative physician, got his clearance from a gynecologist friend. And Golda, just out of the hospital after a gall bladder attack, got her permission only when she told her doctor she'd fast at home anyway if he didn't let her join her comrades.

The next day she packed her suitcase with clothes for an indeterminate stay, stuffed her briefcase with paperwork, and made her way to the Vaad Leumi offices. Reporters from all over the globe followed her up the stairs to the second-floor headquarters where extra desks and hospital beds had been moved in for the strikers. The youngest of the group was forty, and one was a survivor of a concentration camp.

They settled in quickly and, ignoring advice to rest often, tackled the work they'd brought along. Friends and family dropped in frequently, although this was contrary to the rules. The courtyard of the building was soon filled with sympathetic citizens, some of whom sang, some of whom prayed, some of whom stood silently, staring at the windows. The strikers could have a glass of unsweetened tea when their thirst became unbearable, but nothing else could pass their lips. Fortunately for the chain-smoking Golda, cigarettes were not included in that injunction.

By the end of the second day the strikers were resting more and working less. Aboard the *Fede,* and now its sister ship, the *Eliahu Golomb,* the refugees started to collapse from hunger. Solemnly their leaders chalked their numbers on a large board on deck for the benefit of spectators on the pier. Still the British refused to let them sail.

The third day of the strike was Passover, the Jewish holiday commemorating the Exodus from Egypt. Religious law insisted all Jews must eat at the Seder service. This posed a problem for the strikers, one that was ultimately solved by the two chief rabbis in Palestine. That night, when the strikers gathered at the Seder table to hear the story of deliverance, they sipped tea instead of the ritual wine and ate a piece of matzo the size of an olive, instead of the traditional feast. The ancient prayer "Let My People Go" was never so moving, or so pertinent. There was a special Seder prayer for the refugees, too, the concluding one: "Next Year in Jerusalem.'

The refugees gave up and started to eat again on the

fourth day, but the strike in Jerusalem continued. Then the refugees did a remarkable and desperate thing. For each day longer they were held, they announced, ten women and men would climb on deck and, in full view of those on shore, kill themselves. The first ten had already volunteered.

The British let them sail.

The wan strikers in Jerusalem gratefully broke their 104-hour fast with a little bit of milk, mild cheese, and matzo before being taken off to the hospital to recover. *Yishuv* spirits, revived by their success, quickly sank when they found their victory was a hollow one. The British had neatly deducted the number of entry permits for the two ships from that month's quota; thousands would have to wait longer on Cyprus.

But the *Fede* incident did alert the world to the *yishuv's* cause. Why wouldn't the British bend their policy on humanitarian grounds and let the sick and suffering refugees go to the place where people wanted so much to welcome them home?

As this drama reached its climax, the Anglo-American committee announced the recommendations it would make to the newly chartered United Nations. Unanimously the members called for the abrogation of the White Paper and the immediate admission of one hundred thousand refugees. They advised that Jews be allowed to purchase land again, and they suggested that the British mandate be turned over to a long-term U.N. trusteeship. No one was completely happy with the report. The Arabs didn't want any Jews at all in Palestine; the Jews wanted more. One hundred thousand refugees were not enough without a guaranteed quota for the next year. The British swore they couldn't deal with such a large influx of people or with the Arab reprisals that would follow it. Insisting that the report be considered as a whole, they refused to implement any part until all the recommendations could be fulfilled.

The Jews of Palestine were outraged. They'd sacrificed too much now to give in without a fight. At a conference in

Haifa, Golda stated the *yishuv's* attitude toward the mandatory government bluntly:

> We don't want to fight you. We want to build, to construct. We want to enable the remnant of our people, those few who remain, to come here in peace. But if not—then you must understand in the clearest possible manner. We have no choice.

From that moment the *Ma'avak,* the struggle against the British, which until then had been limited to the refugee problem, took on new force. The *yishuv* acted like a sovereign nation now, one that fought back invaders, rescued persecuted citizens, and controlled its borders. Everyone was committed to the fight. When police tried to search a Tel Aviv neighborhood for illegal immigrants, the residents stopped every bus driving through the section and rounded up enough able-bodied citizens to protect the aliens from arrest. The *yishuv* also began to realize that, however abhorrent it might be, some bloodshed would be inevitable if they were to get their state.

In June 1946, one month after the British about-face, the Haganah expanded its subversive activities. On June 16 every bridge, road, and railroad track crossing into Palestine was blown up. The British promptly arrested sixty-two Jews. The underground attacks continued, and on June 29, "Black Saturday," one hundred thousand British soldiers and two hundred police raided kibbutzim, villages, and *yishuv* national offices, arresting twenty-seven hundred more Jews and putting a strict curfew on all towns with any Jewish population. Palestine became a police state.

Among those new prisoners were most of the *yishuv's* leaders. Ben-Gurion, in Europe at the time, could not return without arrest. Everyone else Golda worked with was interned, save Golda herself. All that long Sabbath she sat near her phone, ignoring advice to go into hiding, waiting for the police. She wasn't going to shrink from imprisonment; she would welcome it as a badge of honor. But, for reasons she never knew, no British soldier ever knocked on her door and asked her to accompany him.

She did, however, receive another kind of summons. The head of the *yishuv*'s political office sent her an urgent message just before he was arrested: would she take over for him?

All at once Golda represented all the Jewish organizations in Palestine. She was both minister of labor and foreign minister, in charge of all negotiations with the British. There were other, more experienced contenders for the job, men with years of education and an abundance of political savvy who never became emotional when under attack, as Golda had been known to do. But despite her occasional weepiness, Golda was the best choice. Besides being fluent in English, she instinctively knew how to walk the fine line between diplomacy and provocation with dignity and firmness. And she certainly would need all her skills now, when dealing with an unsympathetic government staffed by callous officers who could quite seriously say things like, "Surely, Mrs. Myerson, if Hitler persecuted the Jews so much, there must have been a reason for it."

Golda's first task was to keep Jewish anger from erupting in more terror. Already there were two groups, the Stern Gang and the Irgun, whose members, tired of self-restraint, were not afraid of killing. She also had to make sure the world knew of the British actions. At numerous press conferences she told reporters about the raids and invited them to photograph the ransacked kibbutzim, the broken desks, and the overturned files with their mutilated papers and pictures.

World opinion was swinging her way when the Irgun struck. On July 23 a bomb concealed in a milk can exploded in Jerusalem's King David Hotel, headquarters of the mandatory government. The blast killed ninety people and wounded forty-five. Immediately condemning the act, Golda urged the rest of the *yishuv* to rise up against these outrages. But it was too late. To the world the Jews had shown themselves to be no better than the British or Arabs they censured.

Golda was now busier than ever before. Fortunately her family obligations were no longer such an emotional drain on her time. Sarah had quit high school and gone to live on a kibbutz in the Negev desert. Menachem still lived with his mother, but he was so busy with his cello and music that the two saw each other only for meals. Golda had by now also accepted the necessity of household help, although she insisted on doing all the cooking for herself, her family, and both invited and unexpected guests.

Her schedule soon proved to be too rigorous. Her gall bladder acted up again, and some nights she collapsed on the couch as soon as she walked in the door. Menachem urged her to take it easy. "You're killing yourself!" he raved.

His mother looked up at him with weary, dark-circled eyes and shrugged. "A lot of people die around fifty," she said.

She nevertheless looked forward to the curfews the British still imposed. That meant a day without visitors. In those quiet hours she could read, or turn a skirt inside out so that the worn, shiny side would no longer show, or simply gaze out the window at the sunlit Mediterranean.

Such days were rare. Curfew or none, Golda could always be reached by telephone. She had to be, for few decisions could be made without her. She consulted with Haganah leaders about all their plans and actions and then stayed awake all night waiting to hear if their missions had been successful. Golda also helped organize Kol Israel, a secret radio station that broadcast the news in Hebrew, Arabic, and English from a different spot each day with equipment that could be quickly disassembled and hidden.

Most of her time was still spent on the refugee problem. The British had added more patrol ships to their fleet enforcing the White Paper, making it almost impossible for the Haganah boats to land undetected. The camps on Cyprus were overflowing; infant mortality there was appallingly high. Golda persuaded the British to alter their "first in, first out" policy and let families with babies and small children emigrate first. Once these people had been deducted from the monthly quotas, the others could leave in the regular order.

Gaining this concession was the easy part. Now Golda had to go to Cyprus and convince the refugees to let others leave out of turn, to prevail on them to wait months or perhaps years longer so that the children might live. It was one of the hardest tasks of her career. Luckily, Golda never worried about the success of an undertaking. If she felt it was right, she took it on, regardless of the outcome. And in this case, she was sure she was right.

Her worst fears about the camps were confirmed when she landed in Cyprus in 1947. Armed British soldiers stood guard around vast barbed-wire enclosures teeming with the very people they had liberated from death camps barely two years before. Malevolent watchtowers marked the corners of the compounds. The inmates crowded into huts and tents clustered on the sand to escape from the scorching sun. Although they could see the Mediterranean from the camp, no one was allowed to go swimming. Nor could one bathe or wash clothes, because all water, even for drinking, was strictly rationed on the island.

But it was the children who tore at Golda's heart. Sickly and listless, they played in the dusty lanes between the tents under the weary eyes of their parents. At one camp two little girls shyly presented Golda with a bouquet of paper flowers; they had never seen a real flower or played on real grass. They moved Golda to be her most persuasive. Some of the refugees agreed to give up their places on the lists to help save the chidlren, and within a month, fifteen hundred little ones and their families set foot on Palestinian soil.

They were only a tiny fraction of the refugee population. It wasn't until 1949 that the last of the fifty-two thousand Jews who had been detained on Cyprus arrived in their homeland, weeping not for joy, but for all their lost years.

Back in Palestine, the situation grew more chaotic. Both the Haganah and the Irgun increased their actions. The British retaliated with more raids, more arrests, and more curfews. The Arabs took advantage of the confusion and stepped up their attacks, secure in the knowledge that the British would look the other way. Life in Palestine was virtually impossible and growing worse every day.

The British suddenly tired of the whole affair and turned the problem over to the United Nations for resolution in February 1947. The fledgling organization, behaving in a time-honored way, dispatched a special fact-finding committee to Palestine in June. As Golda had predicted, the eleven members were all Christians and were entirely ignorant of the situation. "They showed lack of understanding in good measure," she said. But with her help they soon came to know what "all the fuss was about."

Just before they were to return to New York, the committee members got a vivid taste of trouble. British patrol ships stopped a Haganah ship, the *Exodus 1947,* outside Palestinian waters and ordered it to return to Europe. When the captain refused, the British crew attacked the 4,550 passengers of the *Exodus* with clubs and pistols. After a seven-hour fight the *Exodus* surrendered, but the British weren't through. Instead of letting the refugees disembark in Cyprus, they sent them back to D.P. camps in Germany. Not a single country or humanitarian organization protested this insensitive and punitive act. Only Golda, speaking before the Vaad Leumi, dared challenge London. The flow of rescue boats would not stop, she warned. The British might kill Jewish babies, but they couldn't kill Jewish determination. No matter what, Jews would come to their homeland.

Perhaps it was the *Exodus* incident more than anything else that decided the content of the committee's report to the U.N. that September. They called for the partition of Palestine into two independent states: one Arab, one Jewish. The Jews would get six thousand square miles of land, two-thirds of it desert. The Arab state, which would house more people, would be larger and more fertile. Economic ties would bind the new nations, and the city of Jerusalem would become an international city under U.N. administration.

The Arabs immediately rejected the plan; for them, it was all or nothing. But the *yishuv* accepted it. Even though a

Jewish state without Jerusalem was like a "body without a heart," the U.N. recommendation meant that the refugees could start arriving almost at once.

All that autumn the Arabs lobbied furiously at the U.N. to keep the partition plan from being approved. They offered some nations political support, warned others of riots among their Arab minorities, and threatened almost everyone with an oil embargo. The Jews, with nothing to offer anyone except the homeless refugees, had little hope of U.N. endorsement.

On the night of November 29, 1947, Golda sat in her living room, radio turned up, pen and paper before her. The U.N. was making up its mind, and as each vote was taken, Golda carefully tallied it on her pad. Breathlessly she waited and counted. When it was all over, she couldn't believe the result. Thirty-one nations had voted yes, thirteen no, and ten (including Britain) abstained. The United Nations had created a new nation, the first Jewish state in two thousand years. Jews all over the globe rejoiced that the dream of centuries would at last come true.

The very next day the Arabs answered a call to peace with a call to holy war against the Jews, as Golda had known they would. Once again riots raged through the cities, and the Tel Aviv–Jerusalem road became a favorite haunt for snipers and stone throwers. The British, serving their last months in Palestine, stepped in only to search and disarm Jews, even if their only weapon was a three-inch pocket knife.

Not that the *yishuv* had much more. The previous spring the Haganah inventory included eleven thousand out-of-date rifles, two thousand machine guns of varying sizes, and eight hundred mortars. No cannon, no armored cars, no tanks, no radio equipment, no navy, no air force. The *yishuv* had forty-nine thousand soldiers and four days' worth of ammunition against the united and highly sophisticated technology of the Arab states. In the face of continuous and confident promises to throw them into the sea, the Jews were understandably dismayed when the United States declared an arms embargo on the Middle East. The British, honoring treaty obligations, kept supplying Arab arsenals, however.

The *yishuv* knew then that they could have their statehood only if they could fight off six Arab armies at once. Because their future depended on their strength, they began to convert the Haganah and Palmach troops into trained armies. Small bands of men drilled secretly behind high walls of houses, and picnicking teenagers memorized the terrain around their towns. The Jews couldn't afford to ignore the Arab threats. As Golda cautioned them: "I suggest you prepare yourselves as if every word were true. And if it should prove to be false," she added, "we'll survive the disappointment."

While manpower was not a problem, matériel was. The new country had no munitions industry and no money to buy weapons from abroad. Ben-Gurion suggested asking the American Jews for help once more. But they gave so much during the war, objected one minister. The most they could be expected to give would be five million dollars, and the *yishuv* needed at least five times that amount. At this, Ben-Gurion volunteered to go and beg them himself.

Golda spoke up then. Ben-Gurion was needed in Palestine; no one else could do his job. But she could go to America and do the begging for him.

Within hours she was on a plane bound for New York. There had been no time to pack, and so Golda arrived in the middle of a New York winter in a lightweight dress, with no luggage, no winter coat, not even a toothbrush. Two days later she was in Chicago, nervously getting ready to speak before the Council of Jewish Federations and Welfare Funds. She'd be talking to professional fund raisers, very few of whom were Zionists. Golda knew that they'd be hard to convince but that, if she could sway them, the entire Jewish philanthropic network would be open to her.

Golda Myerson was almost fifty years old now. Her face was lined, her hair grayed, her once slender figure thickened. In a simple dark dress, her hair pulled back in a knot, and wearing no makeup, she approached the podium, mentally reviewing the points she wanted to make. As she stood momentarily lost in thought, the audience had a chance to study her. One of them later described her as "looking like a woman out of the Bible."

Suddenly she began to speak, from her heart instead of from her notes, as was her custom. She described the worsening unrest in Palestine, reminding her audience that losing now would mean that "for centuries we are through with the dream of a Jewish people and a Jewish homeland." She continued:

> I have come here tonight to try to impress Jews in the United States with the fact that within a very short period, a couple of weeks, we must have in cash between twenty-five and thirty million dollars. In the next two or three weeks we can establish ourselves. Of that we are convinced. . . .
>
> You cannot decide whether we should fight or not. We will. . . . You can only decide one thing: whether we shall be victorious. . . . That decision . . . has to be made quickly, within hours, within days. And I beg of you, don't be too late. Don't be bitterly sorry three months from now for what you failed to do today. The time is now.

She got her twenty-five million that night. For the next six weeks she toured the country, and everywhere she went the Jews responded generously, taking out bank loans to cover their pledges if they had to. Telegrams from Haganah agents in Europe—asking for funds to buy ammunition or equipment from France or Czechoslovakia—followed her as she traveled through America. To all their requests she was able to respond with an enthusiastic yes. By the time she returned to Palestine in early March 1948, Golda had raised fifty million dollars, ten times the maximum anyone thought she'd get. The yishuv could now face independence with greater confidence.

But Golda had little time to feel proud of her achievement. Two new Arab problems now posed serious questions for the soon-to-be-born state. The first was the slow but steady emigration of Palestinian Arabs to Arab lands. Responding to warnings of impending war, thousands put down their tools and packed their belongings, joining their friends moving slowly along dusty roads to "sympathetic" territory, often just a few miles away. The Jews mounted great publicity to convince them to stay, guaranteeing them equal rights and status in the new state, but the exodus continued.

The second problem was somewhat easier to confront because it involved only one man, King Abdullah of Trans-Jordan. When the partition plan was first announced, Abdullah had assured Golda that he would not join any Arab attack on the Jewish state. Giving her his word as a king and a man, he told her that he believed the Jews had been scattered by divine plan so that they could one day return and revive the Middle East. But as Independence Day drew nearer, the yishuv heard rumors of Abdullah's negotiations with his Arab neighbors. Egypt, Iraq, Syria, and Lebanon rattled their sabers loudly every day; how could Trans-Jordan hope to stay neutral? And by the first of May 1948 it was apparent that neutrality was the most anyone could hope for. The National Council, now the yishuv's provisional government, sent Golda to ask Abdullah to stay out of the coming conflict.

Four days before Independence, Golda and an interpreter drove to the Trans-Jordanian border. Just before crossing into Arab land they stopped the car, and Golda donned the traditional robes and veil of an Arab woman. They would make the rest of the trip disguised as an Arab businessman and his wife. Golda practiced walking in the strange garments for several minutes. She didn't quite master the delicate gait of a Muslim woman, and she was far too fair to be an Arab, but they were relying on Arab custom to help them through: Arab women never spoke in public, and no Arab would dare approach another man's wife.

Abdullah's car met them at the border. At each of ten military checkpoints the car stopped, and Golda pressed herself into a corner of the back seat, trying to be invisible, while her companion and the chauffeur presented the proper documents. After what seemed like an incredibly long ride, they were deposited in front of the private house where the king was to meet them. A door opened, and their host welcomed them into a well-appointed room with comfortable couches and a long, low table with mother-of-pearl inlay.

Abdullah joined them within minutes. Apologizing graciously, he told Golda that his Arab neighbors were pressuring him mercilessly to join the fight against the Jews. To them, remaining neutral was as bad as defending the Jewish state, and Abdullah stood to lose everything unless he fought with his natural allies.

He did try to compromise with Golda, however. He felt the situation might ease if the Jews agreed to postpone statehood and accept a "protected minority" status in his own independent kingdom. After all, he asked, why are you in such a rush?

Slowly Golda shook her head. People who have waited two thousand years to become a nation can hardly be said to be in a hurry, she pointed out as she declined his offer. The Jews would have their state, but now they were certain to have a difficult war with it. Her mission had failed. Soberly and respectfuly she and the king parted, unhappy victims of international politics.

The trip back to Palestine was far more harrowing than the one to Abdullah. Their driver, sensing that his passengers were not what they seemed, grew more frightened at each checkpoint. He didn't want to be caught with two Jews in his car, no matter who they were or whom they'd seen. Finally he stopped, turned around in his seat, and ordered his passengers out. Pointing toward the border, he told them to walk the rest of the way, and then he roared off into the night.

No light from anywhere penetrated the darkness. Their robes tangling around their feet, Golda and the interpreter marched slowly over the hills, praying they wouldn't be spotted and shot by an alert sentry or sniper. They didn't dare talk; each step on the dry grass seemed as loud as a thunderclap. Just before dawn they heard rustling nearby. Suddenly an armed figure stood before them. The two stood terrified until the man smiled and put out his hand. He was a Haganah scout, sent to look for them when they didn't return on time, and with confident strides he led them to safety.

Golda reported to Ben-Gurion and the council right away. Despite the assurance of a terrible war, they all voted to go ahead and declare statehood. Invitations went out to two hundred privileged souls to be present at the birth of Israel at 4:00 P.M., Friday, May 14, 1948, in Tel Aviv.

At two o'clock in the afternoon of Independence Day, Golda left the frantic meetings and preparations and went back to her apartment. She washed her hair, put on her best dress, then lit a cigarette and sat for a while on the terrace. Looking out at the sea, she thought of Menachem, now a music student in New York, and how soon he would be called home to defend his country. She thought of Sarah digging trenches at her kibbutz. She also thought of that frightened child in Pinsk, of the firebrand teenager in Milwaukee, and the tireless pioneer in Merhavia. Soon it would all be in place, and all that she'd worked for and dreamed about for fifty years would become real. The Jews would have a home.

She set out on foot for the Tel Aviv Art Museum where the ceremony was to be held. The crowds along the sidewalk thickened as she neared the modest building, and Golda realized that all their precautions on behalf of secrecy had been in vain. All of Tel Aviv knew what was going on; she prayed the Arab terrorists didn't.

She walked up the steps, past the young Haganah volunteers, and into the hall. The National Council had appropriated two hundred dollars for decorating the building. The sum paid for a crew to scrub the floors, drape the nude paintings, tack blackout curtains over the windows in case of an air raid, and hang a large picture of Theodor Herzl behind the

*Golda Myerson signs Israel's Declaration
of Independence, May 14, 1948.*

T-shaped table where the members of the new government were to sit. It was just fifty years after Herzl's first Zionist Congress.

At precisely four o'clock, Ben-Gurion, head of the council, now dressed for the first time in anyone's memory in a suit and tie, rose to read the Proclamation of Independence. He was cut off, however, by music, as the crowd spontaneously started singing "Hatikvah," the song of hope that was to be the new national anthem. The Philharmonic Orchestra, positioned on the balcony, joined in a few bars late, and the echoing sound filled the building and flowed into the street. When the music finally died, Ben-Gurion read the 979 Hebrew words of the proclamation. He was interrupted by wild applause for the words: "The State of Israel will be open to immigration of Jews from all countries of their dispersion." From that moment on, there were no more Jewish refugees; they all had a home to come to.

Ben-Gurion finished reading and signed his name at the bottom of the large parchment scroll on which the proclamation would later be copied. One by one the thirty-seven other members of the National Council rose to add their names, some coolly, some nervously, some grinning, some weeping. One of the world's oldest nations was being reborn after centuries during which its people, scattered over the earth, had clung to its name, its language, and its faith. "Eretz Israel" would no longer be a phrase in songs and prayers; the land of Israel was now, by act of the United Nations and its citizens, a name that would appear proudly on maps.

Golda was one of the two women to sign the proclamation. Her mind a jumble of memories, anxieties, and fleeting thoughts of Jefferson and Franklin, she was crying so hard when her turn came that someone had to hold the scroll down for her, and guide her hand to the proper spot. She then helped make a nation with her signature.

At midnight the British flag was lowered from the pole in front of the government offices. On Sunday, after the Sabbath, the blue and white Star of David would fly there bravely. With a final salute, the last of the British soldiers departed, leaving the land of Israel to the Israelis.

MAKING
THE DESERTS
BLOOM

6

The infant nation knew only a few hours of peace before it began fighting for its life.

The next day Arab planes flew over the last of the Independence Day celebrations, certain of annihilating their new neighbor. Well equipped and well trained, they expected no resistance from a regular army with only a few thousand odd guns and half a dozen single-engine planes; they knew that most of the arms Golda's money had purchased had not yet arrived.

But the Arab victory was neither swift nor sure. The Israelis commanded hidden reserves. Part of their strength came from knowing that they were not alone in their struggle. Both the United States and the Soviet Union, the postwar superpowers, had recognized Israel and its right to exist almost immediately. But most of that strength came from the Jews' "no alternative" attitude. If they lost this fight, they lost forever.

Rather than wait for the arms shipments, the new government tried to buy more. Once again Golda left a cabinet meeting for the airport with nothing more than her hairbrush, toothbrush, and one clean blouse in her handbag. At United States Customs in New York she proudly displayed the first Israeli passport ever issued, and she mystified officials with one other item in her capacious purse—a long, black veil, the hastily stashed and quickly forgotten souvenir of her visit to King Abdullah.

Even though she had asked so much from American Jews in January, Golda once more presented a blunt plea for help and was again successful. People dug deeper into their pockets and bank accounts so that Israel could win its war for independence.

Disturbing news interrupted Golda's fund raising. She wept when she learned of the surrender of the Jewish section within the walled city of old Jerusalem to Arab forces after three days of continuous shelling and heard how all the Jews left alive in the Old City had been rounded up and exiled to other parts of town. The ancient capital, partitioned and internationalized to ensure equal access for all people to their holy places, was now under Arab occupation. The Jews were forbidden the one spot that represented the heart and soul of Judaism, the Wailing Wall, the last remnant of the great temple that was destroyed when the Romans dispersed the Jews in A.D. 70.

Golda ached to be in Israel while it was struggling so valiantly. But her country needed her elsewhere. The last piece of distressing news she received in America was that she had been named ambassador to the Soviet Union. Because of the USSR's prompt recognition of the state of Israel, this was a very important post. Despite the honor, Golda's first response was, "Why me?" Moscow meant exile to her. But she soon remembered that "one's duty was one's duty—and it had nothing to do with justice," and she accepted the job.

She spent the summer in Israel, gathering her staff and being coached in foreign affairs, protocol, and procedures. The Israeli embassy included twenty-one people, counting the children who were to go along. Golda was glad to be able to take her daughter and new son-in-law as the embassy radio and code experts. In early September, as Israeli forces were finally beginning to push the Egyptians back across the Sinai, Golda's crew boarded the plane for Moscow.

Since the embassy building was not quite ready for them, the group lived in one of Moscow's grand hotels with elegant rooms and crystal chandeliers. Golda was convinced that most of the help there were really agents for the secret police. A few days after her arrival, Golda put on a long black gown, a black turban she detested, and a ten-dollar string of imitation pearls and presented her credentials to the Soviet government. She then settled down to the business of representing Israel.

Her duties included entertaining other diplomats, attending meetings and embassy events, and encouraging trade between Israel and other nations. But another part of her job was to see if there was any hope of reestablishing contact with Russian Jews. Since the Bolshevik Revolution, Judaism had been banned in Russia. Hebrew was a forbidden language; only a few synagogues stayed open for very old citizens; and officials boasted that the entire Jewish population had been assimilated. This seemed likely to Golda who, at her embassy's regular Friday night open house, had never met a Russian Jew, although foreign ones came in droves.

One Friday night Golda and her staff went to the Sabbath services at Moscow's synagogue, sitting quietly among the sparse and aged congregation as prayers for the state of Israel were said. The following week they returned for the Jewish New Year services, but to their amazement they found themselves among thousands of men, women, and children eager to see these messengers from the homeland. And ten days later, on Yom Kippur, the holiest day in the Jewish calendar, fifty thousand Jews, including Red Army officers, jammed the streets around the synagogue, calling Golda's name and reaching out to touch her, despite official warnings in the press to stay away. All Golda could say to the crowd through her tears was, "I thank God you have remained Jews." She was devastated by this demonstration. How could she have believed the government reports? The unity of the Jewish people had survived all attempts to squash it. And even though Golda was never to see these people again (the following week the Soviet government closed all Jewish theaters and presses in another attempt at "assimilation"), she never forgot their show of faith.

Golda remained in Moscow for eight months. When the legation finally moved into its own quarters, Madam Ambassador helped lay the carpets and hang the curtains. She also insisted that *all* staff members sit down to dinner together, and she doled out to everyone the same amount of spending money. The embassy, she felt, should be run like a kibbutz and should be a concrete representation of Israeli ideals. Besides serving as useful socialist propaganda, Golda's arrangement helped her hold on to familiar ways in a very unfamiliar world. Before now she had dealt only with Jews and Jewish problems. Now she could no longer be the Zionist pioneer exclusively. She had to move outward, forge new political, economic, and social ties, and present her country as a full-fledged member of the commonwealth of nations.

Israel was learning to act like a real nation, too, now that it had made a truce with its neighbors. In January 1949, twenty-one political parties vied to fill the one hundred twenty seats in the first Knesset, or parliament. By winning the greatest number of votes and therefore a majority of seats in the Knesset, Golda's party, Mapai, also won the privilege of choosing Israel's first prime minister. David Ben-Gurion assumed these duties, serving not only as the political majority leader in the Knesset but also as chief executive officer of the nation and head of the hand-picked cabinet. One of the first cabinet members he chose was Golda. She became Israel's first minister of labor, and she continued to serve in the cabinet for the next sixteen years.

While more than happy to leave the cold world of Moscow diplomacy, Golda knew that she faced a tremendous

*In Moscow, Golda's appearance at New Year
services drew a throng of Russian Jews, who risked
the condemnation of their government to show
their solidarity with the Jews of Israel.*

challenge. This new position meant formulating and fighting for policy as well as implementing and administering social welfare and public works programs. Her years with the Histadrut had given her considerable expertise in these matters; then, however, she had been dealing with a much smaller community.

But as the news of the birth of Israel spread throughout the world, entire communities of Jews, some isolated for generations, had packed up and set out for the Holy Land. This "ingathering of exiles" brought Jews from as far as China and India, and as close as nearby Arab nations. The Israelis airlifted fifty thousand Yemenite Jews across the Arabian deserts in a move that spanned more centuries than miles, for these Jews had been cut off since the Middle Ages. Operation Ali Baba brought one hundred thousand Iraqi Jews home. In all, during her first two years as labor minister, Golda saw 685,000 immigrants descend on Israel. The newcomers were housed in hastily erected transit camps all over the country, and Golda's first task was to get them settled as quickly as possible.

She soon found work for these newcomers in the fields, groves, and factories near the camps. Where no jobs were available, she created them with an aggressive public works policy designed to train these new citizens, most of whom had arrived with more zeal than skills. The immigrants paved roads and planted forests all across the land, working in crews carefully selected for a mix of national backgrounds, so that barriers between cultural groups broke down as the country was built up.

The new Israelis also needed homes. "Good citizenship and decent behavior cannot develop as long as people live in tents," Golda declared as she pushed a comprehensive housing plan through the Knesset. The government agreed to build thirty thousand one-room structures that each owner would have to finish alone. Besides being an economical approach, this plan served two other functions: it got families out of overcrowded tents quickly, and it taught the homeowners marketable skills. What was soon seen to be a pitifully small number, these units sprang up all over Israel, and Golda had to ask for more.

But the money had run out. Her programs were branded inflationary. Some Israelis were unwilling to bear the austerity and rationing the government had imposed in order to maintain its services and defenses while still absorbing thousands of people a day. Tired of standing in line for hours waiting for three eggs or a soggy package of frozen fish, these citizens argued that immigration should be stopped, or at least limited, until the Israeli economy was stronger.

This attitude horrified Golda. How could anyone think of turning away any Jew who wanted to come? Were they not all immigrants themselves? Greater austerity and greater sacrifice would, she promised, see them through until the mass migration tapered off and these "expensive" immigrants turned into productive citizens. She could see the change starting already during her weekly trips to camps and projects around the nation. Once the newcomers found themselves well fed, well clothed, and well housed, they felt secure, proud, and eager to be useful. The investment Israel made in them could never be too dear, for these people were the hope, strength, and future of the state.

Golda did, however, try to ease the financial strain on the state. She returned to the United States and successfully raised funds for housing just a year and a half after asking for money for guns. But, sensing that inevitably this amazing American pool would evaporate, or at least dry up to a tiny puddle, in 1951 she proposed selling State of Israel Bonds. That way, every gift, or investment, would be repaid. Israel would have cash and some measure of financial independence, and its supporters would have a welcome return on their charity.

Israel's economy improved in 1952. Immigration waned to a mere one thousand a day; bond sales were going well. A reparation agreement with Germany, guaranteeing payment for all Jewish property stolen or damaged by the Nazis, made

In 1955 Golda opened one of the new roads that she helped to create during her term as Israel's labor minister.

$820 million available to Israel. Much of that money went for badly needed heavy machinery, ships, and armaments.

Golda applauded the agreement. It was right that the Germans help build the Jewish state and provide a home for those Jews who had survived their terror. But she herself had other suggestions for ways to use the money. She proposed better government-subsidized housing, pleasant homes with pretty views, instead of cinder-block fortresses in industrial centers. She wanted to create new towns throughout the land where Jews and Arabs could live together, and to link those towns by more of those thoroughfares the Israelis were calling *Goldene Wegen* (Golden Roads) in her honor. She urged permanent vocational training programs for adults and youths and designed welfare legislation to take care of each citizen from birth to death. Golda's paramount concern for people and their problems, as well as her informal, friendly manner, made her a popular minister of labor. She herself said that her seven years on the job were "without doubt, the most satisfying and happiest in my life."

All around her she could see the results of her labors. The deserts bloomed; farms and towns thrived in all corners of the state. But as immigration slowed, so did the projects. By 1956 Ben-Gurion thought that Golda would be more useful in another position and asked her to serve as foreign minister. Like the American secretary of state, she would now be the cabinet adviser on foreign affairs, the one to welcome diplomats, visit heads of state, and represent the government of Israel in the United Nations and the Knesset.

Ben-Gurion's suggestion did not meet with universal approval. Many Israelis saw Golda as a curiosity—half politician, half grandmother—and not as a person who could solve a difficult diplomatic situation. Golda wasn't sure about the change either. Would she be happy leaving the concrete actions and results of social programs for the hazy promises of international relations? Nor was she pleased to learn one very important condition of her acceptance. Ben-Gurion insisted that she and his other ministers all take new Hebrew surnames to symbolize the unity of the reborn nation.

Nevertheless, in 1956 Golda Myerson left the labor department, and Golda Meir (the Hebrew word for "to illuminate") took her desk at the foreign office. She could not waste this chance to forge new friendships for the state and to cement the old.

These fine goals had to wait, however. First she had to meet a new and serious Arab threat. Although Israel, bowing to U.N. requests, had given back much of the land it had captured in 1949, the Arab governments still called for war. Terrorists called *fedayeen* crossed the borders almost daily, raiding kibbutzim and villages, killing anyone who crossed their path. Egypt openly built up gun emplacements and troop camps along its border. And the United Nations, which had helped create this hostility with a partition plan it never firmly backed, looked the other way, letting Israel struggle on its own.

The Arabs had added a new weapon to their arsenal, too. Besides conventional guns and religious fervor, they now had their own refugees. Most of the seven hundred thousand Arabs who had left Palestine in 1948 were still living in detention camps in neighboring nations. These people had no homeland, for the Arab state called for in the partition plan had been swallowed by King Abdullah before it had even been born. The other Arab countries, which had done nothing either to stop Abdullah or to absorb these displaced Palestinians into their own populations, now told these people that Israel was entirely to blame for their misery. The refugee camps became effective breeding grounds for terrorists, as a new generation grew up homeless and hopeless, but full of hate.

When she took office, Golda was one of the few in Israel to realize that the long-simmering situation was coming to a boil. The *fedayeen* raids increased; Soviet arms and equipment poured into Egypt; and Egyptian President Nasser, having already nationalized the Suez Canal, tried to strangle Israel's economy by blockading all its shipping in the Red Sea. When Egypt, Syria, and Jordan signed a military pact in October 1956, Golda was sure that war was imminent.

Rather than wait to be attacked, the Israelis started to mobilize quietly. Two hundred thousand Israelis—army men, artists, archaeologists, and accountants—took their drab uniforms out of their closets and lined up at bus stops to join their regiments. Children practiced running for the air raid shelters, and cautious kibbutzniks started digging a new line of trenches around their compounds.

On October 29 the Israelis struck. Within four days they had crossed the Sinai to the Suez Canal, destroyed arms and equipment, razed the *fedayeen* camps, and knocked out the Egyptian army, taking four thousand prisoners. In another two days they smashed the shipping blockade by capturing the Egyptian fortress of Sharm-el-Sheikh. A week after their sur- prise attack, Israeli forces were in firm control of the Sinai Peninsula and the Gaza Strip, and a few adventurous soldiers climbed Mount Sinai, the first Jews to do so since Moses.

Britain and France took part in the fighting to try to regain control of the Suez Canal by bombing airstrips and landing troops on Egyptian territory. At this point America and the United Nations stepped in, condemning all three countries as aggressors and demanding a cease-fire and complete troop withdrawal. France and England, having failed to retake the canal, complied at once. But Israel refused to move one sol- dier until a U.N. force arrived to keep the peace.

Even then Israel did not withdraw from all occupied Egyp- tian lands. Soldiers would stay in Gaza and Sharm-el-Skeikh, the two places essential to Israel's security and shipping, until the U.N. ensured that the *fedayeen* bases would not be rebuilt and the blockade would not be resumed. Otherwise Israel was in the same danger of destruction it had faced before the war; or perhaps greater, for the Egyptian prisoners had sur- rendered their government-issued copies of Hitler's anti- Semitic *Mein Kampf* along with their rifles.

In March 1957, with U.N. guarantees in hand, an uneasy Golda announced her country's withdrawal of troops from the two tiny strips of land. Golda worried that the U.N. assurances were not worded strongly enough, and she wondered why all the pressure was on Israel to pull out and none on Egypt to make peace. Deeply troubled by the charges of aggression, she reminded the U.N. delegates that:

> *A comfortable distinction has been made: the Arab states unilaterally enjoy the rights of war; Israel has the responsibility of keeping the peace. But belligerency is not a one-way street. . . .*
>
> *The odds against us are heavy; the disparity of forces is great, but we have no alternative but to defend our lives and freedom and the right to security. We desire nothing more than peace, but we cannot equate peace merely with an apathetic readiness to be destroyed. If hostile forces gather for our proposed destruction, they must not demand that we provide them with ideal conditions for the realization of their plans.*

Golda's misgivings came true within a year, when Egyptian troops moved back into Gaza and freed the *fedayeen* while once again the U.N. forces watched silently. The war had done nothing but cost Israel the goodwill of the world. Yet Golda never stopped hoping. Peace will come, she predicted with a sigh, when the Arab leaders get up one morning after a sleepless night spent worrying about their people, ''when saving the lives of their children means more . . . than killing Israelis.''

Until that day, however, she still had other jobs to do. Besides her state visits and U.N. appearances, Golda set up a yearly scientific conference for new nations, at which delegates could share problems and progress. To help women play a more vital role in the development of their countries, she established an international training center for them in Israel.

Golda performed her duties capably and with her own personal style. Although she'd had to accept the fancy residence and chauffeur that went with her job, Golda still preferred to take care of herself whenever she could, and she treated all her employees with warmth, respect, and genuine interest. Not many cabinet ministers washed floors at 2:00 A.M. so as not to offend the cleaning woman, or padded out in a bathrobe to bring tea and cookies to the guards before going to bed. Her informal approach also extended to her meetings with politicians and the press. She frequently held these sessions in her home, interrupting her remarks every so often to ask whether a visitor wanted one lump of sugar or two in his or her tea.

As the only woman cabinet minister, Golda was highly visible and much discussed. When a bomb exploded in the Knesset in 1957 and she was wounded in the leg, her colleagues commended her bravery loudly. Why did they make such a fuss? She hadn't yelled during childbirth, and that had certainly hurt a lot more than grenade fragments in the calf. To her, women were naturally equal to men and should be treated that way. They shouldn't have to be fussed over, or be better than anyone else, or perform miracles every day. When a friend told her that Ben-Gurion, thinking to grant her the highest accolade, had called her "the only man in my cabinet," Golda was nonplussed. Would Ben-Gurion, she wondered, have been flattered if she had referred to him as the only woman in the government?

From 1957 on, Golda paid more attention to the world's developing nations. Her interest was not merely to gain support for Israel outside the Arab world; it had a humanitarian purpose as well. Israel, with its hard-won store of practical and theoretical knowledge, felt it had an obligation to help younger nations laboring toward independence and equality. Looking for ways to guide and encourage countries founded on principles of social justice, Golda stressed that "as long as there is one starving child, Israel is duty bound to help."

The Israeli approach was, like Golda, simple and direct. Israel sent people instead of money and machinery. Doctors, teachers, engineers, and farmers went to tell these countries about the mistakes Israel had made, so that no one would have to repeat them. The Israelis didn't just advise and direct, either; they worked side by side with their trainees. This was often the first time many of these students had ever seen white men work with their hands. Their willingness to get dirty, along with their openness in discussing the hard conditions under which they had gained their experience, made the Israelis much more welcome and more useful than representatives of richer, more powerful nations with unlimited resources.

Israel also invited Africans and Asians to study at its universities, technical schools, factories, and kibbutzim. In all, Golda initiated more than two hundred international-cooperation programs during her tenure as foreign minister and sent more than five hundred advisers throughout the nations of the Third World.

How well her programs had succeeded was obvious during her first African tour in 1958. Everywhere she was greeted with smiles, applause, honors, and eager questions. The Liberian Gola tribe made her a paramount chief. The women of the Zoe tribe admitted her to full membership in their secret society with rites Golda never divulged, so honored was she by the gesture. In Ghana she danced the hora with government officials. At each stop she discussed everything from practical socialism to women's rights, wasting no opportunity to remind her listeners that while nothing ever comes easily, it *is* possible to jump across centuries of tradition in the space of one generation. The Africans soon recognized her as a person who said the same thing in public and in private, and she became for them a symbol of honesty and trust. By the time she got to Nigeria, one official was able to tell her that her ministry had the wrong name. It isn't a foreign ministry, he said. "To us it is a friendly ministry."

Golda also toured Asia and Latin America, but she often found herself back in the United Nations. In May 1960, for example, Israeli Nazi-hunters found Adolf Eichmann, the chief architect of Hitler's "final solution," hiding in Argentina. They kidnapped him and brought him to Israel for trial. Argentina, outraged at this violation of its jurisdiction, went to the U.N. and demanded Eichmann's return. In simple words Golda

On her African tour as foreign minister,
Golda danced the traditional hora
with government officials and students.

answered Argentina's appeal, apologizing for the rough way the arrest had been made, but affirming Israel's right to try him. It was not just to punish a murderer, she said, but to break the world's "collective amnesia" and show future generations the horrors and evils of Naziism. "To my sorrow," she said, "there are still people who do not understand that those Jews who were killed in the gas chambers will have been the last Jews ever to die without defending themselves." The U.N. agreed with her explanation, and Eichmann was hanged in Israel in 1961.

Golda also had to address that body about the stubborn Palestinian Arab refugee problem. A Syrian conference on refugees in 1957 had rejected any possible U.N. solution that did not call for Israel's annihilation as "a desecration of the Arab people and an act of treason." The Arab nations still kept these people, whose numbers had swelled after the Suez war, in big camps, supporting them with U.N. funds while demanding that they be returned to their ancient lands. Golda charged that the refugees were deliberately kept in camps to provide a constant source of Israeli victims for Arab propaganda. Israel had taken some responsibility for them: it released their bank accounts, offered them some compensation for their land, and even reunited some families. But Golda was firm in refusing to take back all the Palestinians who claimed a right to return. "This would not be taking refugees back," she said. "This is an army, bent on destroying us." Instead of repatriation, she urged the U.N. to consider resettlement, rehabilitation, and compensation for the refugees, so that they could get out of the camps and on with their lives. Once again, her suggestions fell on deaf ears.

In the early summer of 1961, Golda took time from her busy schedule to give a gala party. The occasion was a reunion of the *Pocahontas* contingent that had arrived in Palestine with her forty years before. Eight of the original group came with their families, and children and grandchildren of the others came, too. It was a night for song and talk, for new friendships and fond memories. The younger generations reflected the Israeli melting pot in their faces, spoke Hebrew easily, and listened in amazement to their elders' pioneering songs and stories. To them, a Jewish state was a matter of fact, not a miracle. Golda passed among her guests in her home, recalling the Zionist ideals that had brought them halfway around the world, reflecting on the courage and determination that had kept them there, and marveling that, with her help, the dream of a few had come true for so many.

WE HAVE NO ALTERNATIVE

7

Golda kept trying to retire. Many of her contemporaries had left the government, and she wanted to also, before she got too old to be useful. But in 1963 Ben-Gurion's successor, Levi Eshkol, begged her to stay on and help start his administration. Golda reluctantly agreed to serve as foreign minister for a few more years; then she would definitely return to private life. After all, she was nearly seventy years old. Her health was weakening; lately she'd been in and out of hospitals with complaints ranging from pneumonia to phlebitis to kidney stones to sheer exhaustion. Severe migraines plagued her at home. Golda also wanted to spend more time with her ailing sister Sheyna. And besides, she'd worked for nearly forty years, never taking a vacation or putting her own wishes first, and she deserved time off.

Looking forward to the luxuries of reading, relaxing, and going to the movies, in 1966 Golda packed up her papers, closed the door to her office, and rode home on the public bus. She didn't go to the official residence, but to her half of the house she shared with her son Menachem and his family.

Golda was a grandmother five times over now. Sarah's two children lived on the same Negev kibbutz that had been growing steadily since Sarah moved there in the 1940s. Menachem's three sons were right next door, however, and several times a day would tear through the common garden to see what their grandma had in her refrigerator.

Golda's retirement was not total, of course. She remained a member of the Mapai party and kept her seat in the Knesset. Meetings and briefings interrupted her days, for younger politicians and elder statesmen still valued her opinions and advice. And after one month, just as Golda was getting used to having large blocks of time to call her own, she went back to work.

Mapai was still Israel's largest party; it had selected Eshkol and dictated major policies and decisions. But since the early 1960s splinter groups and factions had challenged the unity of the party, sapping its strength and threatening its effectiveness. Golda seemed to be the only one with the experience, talent, and time to silence the squabbling, and she was glad to become Mapai's secretary-general. Pleased to be able to help when she felt "the future of the labor movement was at stake," Golda's return to the office was also motivated by her boredom with the slower pace her life was taking.

Once again she was a part-time grandmother and a full-time politician. Her appointment book recorded dozens of conferences and caucuses; her secretary arranged speaking engagements for her all over the country. By concentrating on Israel's accomplishments and progress, on common needs and dangers, Golda began to restructure Mapai's political alliances. Slowly her message of reconciliation sank into the heads of party members.

She used her position in other ways, too. She still sought to strengthen the bonds between Israel and world Jewry, and she tried to encourage more Jews, especially Americans, to emigrate. And she wielded such influence in the government that her opponents took to calling her "the power behind Eshkol's throne."

Eshkol and his cabinet called on Golda more and more as the spring of 1967 blossomed toward summer. Arab terrorist attacks increased in number and ferocity. Arab soldiers, armed with the latest in Soviet weaponry, lined up at Israel's borders. Egypt tried blockading Israeli shipping again and kicked the U.N. forces out of Sharm-el-Sheikh. Golda thought sadly of the 1956 Sinai campaign and of Israel's unwilling concessions as, ten years later, she once again heard Arab voices crackling through the radio, promising to wipe Israel off the face of the earth.

One thing Jews had learned during their bitter history was to believe anyone who threatens to kill them. When none of the seventeen U.N. members that had guaranteed Israel's free shipping in 1957 protested Egypt's moves, the Israelis understood that, once again, they'd have to look out for themselves. With Washington, Paris, and London urging patience and restraint, Tel Aviv ordered a secret, slow mobilization. Regular soldiers and reservists went on alert. Citizens swept out air raid shelters and stocked them with canned goods, bottled water, and blankets. Housewives hung blackout curtains. Schools closed so that children could help dig trenches and fill sandbags; older students filled in for those now in uniform. Hotels evicted their tourists and turned themselves into hospitals, and rabbis solemnly consecrated park land for cemeteries.

By the end of May, when the tension of waiting was almost palpable, the Israelis got unexpected aid. Jews from abroad arrived to volunteer for the army and auxiliary services. Prompted by the realization that if Israel were to disappear, no Jew anywhere would ever feel free again, these young people pledged their lives to the survival of the homeland. Golda was particularly delighted by the American contingents and urged them to stay on afterward. She figured that if they were willing to die there, they should be thrilled to live there.

Early on June 1, Eshkol called an emergency cabinet meeting. Having concluded that Israel must strike first in order to push the Arabs back, he appointed Moshe Dayan defense minister, and on the following Monday, June 5, the armed forces went to work. The air force quickly wiped out Egyptian airfields and cleared the way for land attacks. The army— carried across the Sinai in buses, milk wagons, ice cream trucks, and any other vehicles they could get—drove the Egyptians out of the desert and into surrender in four days. At the same time, other troops headed north and east, capturing Syria's concrete bunkers on the Golan Heights and pushing Jordan's armies back across the river. In hand-to-hand fighting the Jews recaptured Jerusalem and ruled the whole city again after nineteen centuries. The tiny nation's hand, offered so long in peace, had finally clenched into a fist and smashed its enemies.

Golda, who had spent each night of the war sitting on a hard kitchen chair in an air raid shelter, smoking and watching over her companions, cursed that once again she would have to leave her country in its time of danger. But she had long-standing speaking engagements in the United States she could not ignore. On the fifth day of fighting she started out for the airport, directing her driver to make one detour. She could not leave the country without visiting the Wailing Wall.

Golda hadn't been there since she and Morris first moved to Jerusalem from Merhavia. Then it had glowed in the afternoon sun, spreading peace over those who prayed at its stones. Following ancient custom, Golda had scribbled a prayer for happiness on a scrap of paper and stuck it into a chink. How different the Wall was now:

> There was a table . . . on it were . . . submachine guns. . . . Four or five parachutists, with prayer shawls over their uniforms, were praying at the Wall. . . . Every once in a while another one would come running in. This was their first chance to get to the Wall . . . and these heroes, they wept like babies. . . . And then, it was so natural—I took a piece of paper. This time I wrote Shalom, peace, and put it in the Wall.

And one of them—he wept near the Wall as though he would leave his heart there. And he turned around, still with his machine gun, and saw me. I'm not sure that he knew who I was. At any rate, I didn't know him, certainly. All of a sudden he just walked up to me, put his head on my shoulder, and really wept like a baby. . . . I also cried a little bit, I must admit.

She arrived in New York to find American Jews rejoicing over the Israeli victories. Everywhere she looked she saw proud headlines, blue and white Israeli flags, and a full-color poster showing an Orthodox Jew in a phone booth, ripping open his shirt to reveal a Superman costume underneath. But even though she was heartened by their relief that the Israeli death sentence had been lifted, Golda had to remind her euphoric audiences that "We don't want wars even when we win. The Israelis have no joy in killing, no joy in shooting, no joy in winning wars. The Israeli soldiers [are] the saddest victorious army in history."

Golda had lived too long to count on this being the war that would bring lasting peace. During that long summer, while Israelis counted and buried and mourned their dead, Egypt purchased new arms cheaply from the Soviet Union. The world again raised its voice to condemn Israeli aggression and to demand the return of all the land it had just gained, despite Israeli protests that those territories were vital to its security. It was like the Sinai War all over again.

But this time the Israelis were more stubborn. They would not withdraw without peace and secure, defensible, recognized borders. If they gave the land back first, what incentive would the Arabs have to negotiate? Yielding in 1956 had sent another generation to war. With her usual directness, Golda voiced the way many Israelis interpreted world opinion:

A wonderful people, these Israelis! They win wars every ten years, whatever the odds. And they have done it again. Fantastic! Now that they have won this round, let

them go back where they came from, so that Syrian gun-
ners on the Golan Heights can again shoot into the kib-
butzim, so that Jordanian Legionnaires on the towers of
the Old City can again shell at will, so that the Gaza strip
can again be a nest for terrorists, so that the Sinai Desert
can again become the staging ground for Nasser's divi-
sions.

No, this time there'd be no concessions. No one would draw any maps or surrender one inch of land until the Arabs them-selves came to the peace table.

Leaving treaty talks to others, Golda retired again in 1968. She had engineered a strategic coalition of labor inter-ests in a reborn Israel Labor party, had served as its head until she was sure it was viable, and then she escaped once more from "the tyranny of her appointment book."

For several months Golda was a private citizen. She baby-sat, read novels, and shopped in the markets like any housewife. While she maintained her ties with the govern-ment, she was no longer the constant adviser she'd been before the Six-Day War, and she gradually got used to a life without heavy responsibilities.

But when Levi Eshkol died suddenly in February 1969, Golda's idyll vanished once again. With general elections not scheduled until October, the party had to propose an interim prime minister. The two most likely candidates were so busy fighting with each other that to choose either would lead to disaster. Clearly a neutral third figure was needed—and whom could the party turn to but Golda? Her popularity might not be as high as it once was (after all, she'd been out of office quite a while), but her political colleagues admired the decisiveness and persuasiveness she'd shown in forming the new coalition. Besides, they figured, six months in office would be a fitting tribute for Golda's lifetime of service.

Golda hesitated. She wasn't sure she wanted to be prime minister at all, let alone a lame duck. Pointing out that while being seventy was not a sin, it was no joke either, she hinted that she might be too old for the job. But in the end, as always, she agreed.

The only real obstacle to her appointment came from Orthodox Jews who charged that, according to Jewish law, no woman may head a nation. Golda's supporters, arguing that she hadn't been chosen to lead the country, just her party, overcame this opposition, and on March 17 she was elected by a tremendous margin in the Knesset. Golda was now one of the three women prime ministers in the world. In her maiden speech, she admitted to the Knesset that she was filled with "awe and trepidation and endless doubts."

But anyone seeing her behind her big wooden desk would never have guessed at her reluctance. Once again putting aside her personal life, she took over the country with a sure, firm hand, secure enough in her position to reassure her male colleagues jokingly that she would grant them absolute equality. Within weeks she had won the nation's confidence, and in October she and her party won half the seats in the Knesset, an astonishing feat in a sixteen-way race.

Golda's cabinet represented a coalition of ninety percent of the electorate; the press called it her "wall-to-wall cabinet." Her government had inherited many problems. One was religion. No one had yet devised a comfortable way to keep Judaism out of the Jewish state's secular affairs; separation of church and state, while essential, seemed almost impossible. There was also the problem of discrimination against Oriental Jews, so different in coloring and culture from the descendants of European stock. Incredibly high inflation and labor disputes completed a grim picture that was brightened only by the prospect of rising exports, expanding social services, and booming tourism.

The major problem facing Golda's administration, however, was still Arab hostility. The Arabs who had always lived in Israel were not the trouble; they knew they were better off than other Arabs in the Middle East. Arabic is the second of Israel's official languages; both Arab men and women can vote; Arab children enjoy the benefits of compulsory education to the age of fifteen. But after the 1967 War, Israel governed one million more Arabs in the occupied territories. Despite efforts to improve their living conditions, extending the miracles of permanent housing, electricity, and plumbing to people who had always lived in primitive poverty, the Israelis quickly found that they had adopted a population that hated them.

Neighboring Arab states complemented and encouraged this new internal strife. Not having signed a peace treaty with Israel in 1967, they were now trying to wear that nation down with a war of attrition, relying on terror and surprise instead of pitched battles to defeat their enemy. Jet planes would sometimes scream through Israeli skies and bomb desert kibbutzim. School children in the town of Ma'alot were massacred. Israeli diplomats died opening letter bombs in offices all over the world. The terror extended to airplane hijackings, sniper attacks, and even the murder of Israeli athletes competing at the Munich Olympics in 1972.

Israel, refusing to be drawn into another total war, limited its response to retaliatory strikes at Arab bases. Golda made many clandestine trips and held many secret meetings to negotiate a truce, all to no avail. The Arabs just complained louder about Israel's aggressive bombings. The world once again tried to impose its solutions, but Golda held out for peace through direct negotiations.

She had little faith left in the United Nations and even less in its peacekeeping abilties. She was sure the Soviet Union didn't really want peace in the Middle East for fear of losing its access to oil. Who else could Israel turn to? Since both President Kennedy and President Johnson had personally assured her that they would let nothing happen to Israel, in 1969 Golda traveled to America to get the same assurances from Richard Nixon. In twelve days of talks she captured United States support and purchased American planes. She put Israel's position very plainly: ''We intend to remain alive. Our neighbors want to see us dead. This is not a question that leaves much room for compromise.''

Heartened by her American reception, Golda agreed to a cease-fire with Egypt in June 1970. Her personal doubts, born of long experience, were echoed by her vocal opponents in the Knesset. But she had a responsibility to seek peace, and America had promised to ensure that Egypt would not restock its arsenal during the temporary lull. But two weeks after the papers were signed, Israeli reconnaissance planes photographed new Soviet missiles and detection devices in place on Egyptian airfields.

That was the last straw for the Israelis. There would be no more agreements until the cease-fire violations were fixed. In a speech at the U.N. that October, Golda told the delegates gathered to celebrate the organization's twenty-fifth anniversary, that this episode was just one in a series of transgressions that halted all steps toward peace. The Middle East needed the "building of faith and not the breach of faith." As Golda finished speaking she looked around the hall for a sympathetic face. She heard some polite applause from the back of the chamber, but watched the Arab members conspicuously ignore her words, just as they had all the others she had spoken from that platform over the years. Nothing, not even Nasser's death and the succession of the more moderate Anwar Sadat, had softened the Arab position.

Golda returned home more convinced than ever of the need for a strong defense. From now on each terrorist attack would be answered with heavier counterviolence. It was time to throw out the old Haganah policy of self-restraint; Israel was through with gimmicks, too. Golda would tolerate no more observers, U.N. forces, demilitarized zones, or armistices. Nothing had worked. She understood, although the world would not, that the real issue in this undeclared war was not some barren land, but the very right of Israel to exist. And Golda woud never give that up.

But even through constant raids and unexpected violence, Golda had to give some attention to Israel's other concerns. Social programs still had to run smoothly; labor problems still had to be solved. To her sorrow, Golda found herself siding against the workers when she cracked down on strikers for making what she considered unreasonable demands. Israel could not afford to have anyone sitting idle when its future was at stake, but neither could it afford to pay ever-increasing wages when it had to spend so much on defense.

Despite her reputation for cooking up cabinet decisions in her kitchen (a snide reference to the meetings she often held in her home), Golda ran her government the way an old-fashioned schoolmarm ran her classroom. She gave her ministers assignments, encouraged their debate, and never hesitated to stop anyone who rambled too far from the matter at hand. Thanks to her independent spirit, she could make firm decisions, but she also knew how to engineer a compromise with opposing views. Intuition, insight, and compassion merged with practicality, determination, and strength to make Golda a vital leader whose energy and purposefulness inspired those same traits in others.

After nearly four years in office Golda began to tire of hearing that Israel should give in to the Arabs, and of repeating that peace would come only with talk. She had watched, horrified, as other nations acceded to terrorist demands, and now, in May 1973, she was not surprised to learn that the Egyptians and Syrians were again massing troops at their borders.

Were they anticipating another Israeli strike, perhaps a forceful response to the war of attrition? But Israel had no plans to fight. All that summer, as more Arabs joined their comrades in arms, Israeli soldiers followed their normal routines, thinking of the coming Jewish New Year instead of war.

It wasn't until early October, when the Knesset got word that the Soviet advisers were suddenly leaving Syria, that Golda realized something was wrong. Intelligence reports assured her that there was no real sign of imminent war, but she put the army on alert anyway. Her cabinet urged her not to mobilize. It was expensive and unnecessary. Besides, Israel certainly couldn't make another preemptive strike without losing all its remaining allies. The best thing to do, they counseled, would be to sit tight and wait for the Arabs to go home. Golda followed their advice, but with a heavy heart. She never forgave herself for not trusting her instincts and calling up the army.

For the Arabs struck the next day, on the holiday of Yom Kippur, when virtually all Israel had stopped to pray and fast. The Egyptians crossed the Suez Canal, and the Syrians bombarded the Golan Heights while the Israelis scrambled from their homes and synagogues, pulling on their uniforms and dog tags as they rushed to find their units. The Israeli delay was nearly fatal, for it took several days, a massive American airlift of supplies, and twenty-five hundred lives to push the invaders back to where they came from. This second-longest war in Israel's history ended abruptly when, seeing that more fighting would lead to its Arab allies' defeat, the Soviet Union joined the United States in calling for a cease-fire. Golda agreed to this in late October, just before a truly conclusive Israeli victory, hoping to avoid more bloodshed by stopping the hostilities.

Golda's countrymen were enraged by her action. They had wanted to win this war decisively. And the cease-fire was broken almost at once. The Arabs had done so well with their surprise attack that they were sure they'd won the war, and they held Israeli prisoners ransom for Israeli concessions. A second, more successful cease-fire, based on Egyptian and Israeli promises to negotiate, took effect in November. Despite world pressure and despite the strangling Arab oil embargo on Israel's friends, Golda would neither concede land nor move from her position that the war could end only with a directly negotiated peace treaty.

As the autumn wore on, Israel found itself deserted by more and more allies. The world's dependence on oil forced many governments, including sympathetic socialist ones, to decide that a healthy economy was more important than allegiance to a tiny nation that had no oil. The African countries Israel had helped, denounced the "imperialist Zionists." And although the American secretary of state, Henry Kissinger,

Prime Minister Golda Meir visited Defense Minister Moshe Dayan and Israeli troops on the Golan Heights during a cease-fire in the 1973 war.

was guiding negotiations among Israel and Syria and Egypt, it seemed to many Israelis that he held the Arab interests nearer to his heart than theirs.

The country's mood was bitter and black. Families, worn out with waiting for news of sons and husbands and fathers and brothers missing in action, turned angrily on the government. Accused of irresponsibility in not preparing for the attack, Golda and her cabinet were also blamed for the enormous number of casualties, for "selling out" with a premature cease-fire, and for not stopping the guerrilla terrorists who struck again even after the armies had gone home. Distressed by public and party protests, Golda offered to resign before her term expired in December. The Knesset urged her not to quit, and, to her surprise, on December 31 the party again swept the polls, returning Golda to another five-year term.

But the victory was a hollow one. Sharing her nation's sense of loss and bitterly hurt by being used as the "butt of her people's agony," Golda knew by April 1974 that she could no longer continue in office. Let others try to please both hawks and doves; she didn't want to go on without the complete backing of all her colleagues and country. She ended fifty years of public service on June 4, after announcing the truce with Syria and welcoming home the first returning Israeli prisoners of war. She showed the new prime minister, Yitzak Rabin, around the office, and then Golda went home, this time for good.

Golda Meir in retirement was like a queen in exile. Her voice still commanded authority in the Labor party. Government officials continued to seek her out for information and advice. She always invited visiting heads of state to her home for tea and cakes. In fact, she was working and traveling as much as ever. Golda wrote her autobiography, made a sentimental pilgrimage to her elementary school in Milwaukee, and was on hand to welcome Egyptian President Sadat when he made his historic visit to Jerusalem in 1977. There was less time than she thought to spend with her family, read, or even straighten up her bookshelves.

Golda remained an active and vocal force in Israeli affairs until, complaining of spinal pains and jaundice, she entered the hospital in October 1978. She never left it. On December 8, at the age of eighty, Golda died. Only after her death did her doctors reveal her awful secret. For the past fifteen years, during two wars and her term as prime minister, Golda had suffered from cancer of the lymph glands. Through the torment of the illness and its treatment, Golda had carried on with her job, refusing to let mere disease stop her before her work was done.

Although she did not live to see it secure, Golda did see Israel established and flourishing. During a lifetime as dramatic as any screenplay, she had always done what she could for the Jewish state. As a young girl she'd raised money and preached the Zionist creed to American compatriots. As a young bride she'd joined a kibbutz, helping to build the homeland with her hands. Even the demands of motherhood could not compete with her dream of nationhood. Fortified by her faith in Judaism and Zionism and motivated by her love for Israel, Golda committed herself to the service of her country and shaped the course of history.

When she returned from America in 1948 with the fifty million dollars for arms, David Ben-Gurion thanked her by saying, "Someday when our history is written, it will be said that there was a Jewish woman who got the money that made the state possible." Over the years Golda became more than Israel's fund raiser. A member of that earnest generation of Russian-born Jews who built the nation, Golda's single-mindedness and strength made her the champion of her people. Never forgetting the lessons of history, she refused to let Jews be at anyone's mercy ever again. She prayed for peace, but when her prayers were not answered, she prepared for war, rather than let her people disappear.

Golda intended to die a kibbutznik; she never planned to be prime minister. It happened, she said, "because that's how it was." She had done what her country asked. In doing so, she was a symbol to men and women all over the world. Women saw her as an example of all they could accomplish.

In her unceasing efforts for social justice, she represented the ethical teachings of Judaism. To the developing nations of the Third World, she personified genuine concern and generous aid.

But above all, Golda was the voice of peace and understanding. She was sure the day would come when Israel and its neighbors would live in harmony instead of discord. "I refuse to believe," she said, "that Egyptian mothers in the Nile Valley are giving birth to their children . . . for the glorious ideal that they will go off to war and fight the Israelis and who knows whether they will come back." To her, life was what mattered most, and, convinced that it mattered most to Arabs, too, she was able to envisage a future "for friendship, peace, and cooperation between our neighbors and ourselves."

Golda considered her life blessed for having been able to see her grandchildren grow up free Jews in their own country. When she first came to Palestine, neither she nor anyone else expected to see an independent Jewish state during her lifetime. But after nearly sixty years of loving labor, she could look back and say that all the hardships, struggles, and sacrifices were worth it. "People who don't get excited, I just can't understand," she'd say. "My God! A Jewish state! What a wonderful and thrilling thing!"

FOR FURTHER READING

*Agress, Eliyahu. *Golda Meir: Portrait of a Prime Minister*. New York: Sabra Books, 1969.

Ben-Gurion, David. *Israel: Years of Challenge*. New York: Holt, Rinehart & Winston, 1963.

*Comay, Joan, and Pearlman Moshe. *Israel*. New York: Macmillan, 1964.

*Davidson, Margaret. *The Golda Meir Story*. New York: Scribner, 1976.

*Dobrin, Arnold. *A Life for Israel: The Story of Golda Meir*. New York: Dial Press, 1974.

*Levin, Meyer. *The Story of Israel*. New York: Putnam, 1966.

*Of interest to younger readers

*Mann, Peggy. *Golda: The Life of Israel's Prime Minister.* New York: Coward, McCann, & Geoghegan, 1971.

Meir, Golda. *My Life.* New York: Putnam, 1975.

*Noble, Iris. *Israel's Golda Meir.* New York: Julian Messner, 1972.

Syrkin, Marie. *Golda Meir: Woman with a Cause.* New York: Putnam, 1963.

Wiesel, Elie. "Golda at 75." *Hadassah Magazine,* January 1973.

INDEX

Italicized page numbers indicate photographs.

Abdullah, King of Transjordan, 75–76, 90
Africa, 94, *95*, 109
Aliyah, 5–6, 23
American Jewish Congress, 18
American Jews, 5–6, 8–20, 23–30, 73, 82, 103
Anti-Semitism: late nineteenth-century European, 5; Nazi Germany, 53–54, 56–61, 64, 94, 96; Russian, 1–2, 5, 6–7
Arab League, 63
Arabs, 41, 89; hostility towards Palestine, 54–56, 63, 70–82, 90–92, 96, 101–104, 105–111. *See also names of countries*
Ashkenazim, 14
Auschwitz, 57

Balfour Declaration, 27–28, 42

Ben-Gurion, David, 23, 57, 67, 73, 77, 79, 85, 89, 93, 112
"Black Saturday," 67
B'nai B'rith, 18

Concentration camps, 57, 58

Dachau, 57
Dayan, Moshe, 101–102, *110*
Dreyfus case, 5

Economy, 42, 53, 55, 86–87, 89, 105
Egypt, 33, 75, 90–92, 101–103, 106–109, 111
Eichmann, Adolf, 94, 96
Eshkol, Levi, 99, 100, 101, 104
Exodus incident, 71

Fedayeen raids, 90–92
Fede hunger strike, 64–66
Fishing industry, 52–53
France, 91; Jews in, 4, 5

Gaza Strip, 91, 92, 104
Germany: Nazi persecution of
  Jews in, 53–54, 56–61, 64, 94,
  96; reparation agreement with
  Israel, 87, 89
Golan Heights, 102, 109, *110*
Goldene Wegen, 89
Great Britain, 41, 56, 91; and Bal-
  four Declaration, 27–28; and the
  White Paper, 56–60, 62, 64–71

Haganah, 55, 59–60, 67, 69, 70,
  72, 107
Hebrew, 34, 43, 63–64, 83, 89–90
Herzl, Theodore, 5–6, 77, 79
Histadrut, 38, 42–43, 49–60
Hitler, Adolf, 53–54, 56–61, 64
Holocaust, 53–61, 64, 94, 96
Hovevi Zion, 4

Immigration, Jewish: to America,
  5–6, 8–20; to Palestine, 31–34,
  56–60, 62–71, 87, 89
Independence Day, 77, *78*, 79, 81
Iraq, 75
Irgun, 68, 70
Israel: Arab hostility towards, 72–
  83, 90–92, 96, 101–104, 105–
  111; creation of, 72–79; German reparation agreement with,
  87, 89; Jewish immigration to,
  87, 89; Knesset of, 84, 86–111;
  U.S. aid to, 73–74, 81, 87, 101,
  106–107, 109. *See also* Jews;
  Palestine; Zionism

Jerusalem, 39, 68, 71–72, 82, 102
Jewish Labor Federation, Palestine, 42
Jews: American, 23–30, 73, 82,
  103; French, 4,5; German, 53–
  54, 56–61, 64, 94, 96; Oriental,
  105; Russian, 1–2, 5, 6–7, 83–
  84, *85*. *See also* Israel; Palestine; Zionism

Jordan, 90, 102

Kibbutzim, 23–24, 35, *36*, 37–39
Kissinger, Henry, 109–110
Knesset, 84, 86–111
Kol Israel, 69

Labor Zionist party, 6, 26, 28
Lebanon, 75

Mapai party, 57, 85, 100
Meir, Golda, *19, 22, 29, 36, 47,
  78, 85, 88, 95, 110*; as ambassador to Soviet Union, 82–84,
  85; birth of, 2; childhood of, 2–
  4, 7–25; death of, 112; as foreign minister, 89–97, 99–104;
  immigration to Palestine, 31–34;
  marriage of, 28; as minister of
  labor, 84, 86–90; Moetzet Hapoalot work of, 42–46, 48, 49;
  Pioneer Women work of, 45–46,
  47, 48; as prime minister, 104–
  111; retirement of, 99–100, 104,
  111; rise as Histadrut leader,
  38–60; and World War II, 58–61
Merhavia, 35, *36*, 37–39
Mifdeh, 51
Moetzet Hapoalot, 42–46, 48, 49
Munich Olympics, 1972, 106

Nachshon, 52–53
Nazi Germany, 53–54, 56–61, 64,
  94, 96
Nuremberg Laws, 53
Nuremberg trials, 64

Oriental Jews, 105
Ottoman Empire, 4, 27

Palestine: Arab hostility towards,
  54–56, 63, 70–82, 90–92, 96,
  101–104, 105–111; and early
  Zionism, 4–6, 23–53; Histadrut
  in, 38, 42–43, 49–60; Jewish

immigration to, 31–34, 62–71, 87, 89; Jewish state created in, 72–79; kibbutzim, 23–24, 35, *36*, 37–39; and Nazi Germany, 53–61, 64, 94, 96; post-World War II, 61–113. *See also* Isreal; Jews; Zionism
Passover, 65
Petach Tikva, 4
Pioneer Women, 45–46, *47*, 48
Poalei Zion, 6, 26, 28
Pogroms, 1–2, 5, 6–7

Sadat, Anwar, 107, 111
Seder, 65
Shipping industry, 52–53
Sinai Peninsula, 91–92, 102, 104
Soviet Union, 81, 103, 106–107, 109; anit-Semitism in, 1–2, 5, 6–7; Golda Meir as ambassador to, 82–84, *85*; Jews in, 1–2, 5–7, 83–84, *85*
Stern Gang, 68
Suez Canal, 90, 91, 109
Syria, 75, 90, 102, 108, 111

Talmud Torah, 18
Tel Aviv, 25, 33, 34, 52–53, 56
Third World, 94, 113
Tourism, 49–50
Tradition, Jewish, 18, 28, 52

Transjordan, 75–76

Unemployment, 50–51
United Nations, 66, 71–72, 90–92, 94, 96, 101, 106
United States, 72; European Jewish refugees in, 57; Israel aided by, 73–74, 81, 87, 101, 106–107, 109

Vaad Hapoel, 49–60

Wage scales, 50
Wailing Wall, 82, 102–103
White Paper, 56–60, 62, 64–71
World War I, 25, 26, 27, 55
World War II, 58–61
World Zionist Congress, 1897, 5–6

Yiddish, 14, 18
Yishuv, 25
Yom Kippur, 83
Youth Aliyah, 54

Zionism: American, 23–30; and Balfour Declaration, 27–28, 42; early, and Palestine, 4–6, 23–53; late nineteenth century, 4–6; and Nazi Germany, 53–61, 64, 94, 96; *See also* Israel; Jews; Palestine

92
Mei

Golda Meir

MAY 1 2 1989	DATE DUE	
MAY 1 9 1989		